Vassilis Nitsiakos

Peklari

Balkan Border Crossings

Contributions to Balkan Ethnography

edited by :

The Border Crossings Network
publications series

Monograph III

LIT

Vassilis Nitsiakos

PEKLARI

Social economy in a Greek village

LIT

Bibliographic information published by the Deutsche Nationalbibliothek
The Deutsche Nationalbibliothek lists this publication in the Deutsche Nationalbibliografie; detailed bibliographic data are available on the Internet at http://dnb.d-nb.de.

ISBN 978-3-643-90783-7

A catalogue record for this book is available from the British Library

Klosbachstr. 107
CH-8032 Zürich
Tel. +41 (0) 44-251 75 05 Fax +41 (0) 44-251 75 06
E-Mail: zuerich@lit-verlag.ch http://www.lit-verlag.ch

Distribution:

In the UK: Global Book Marketing, e-mail: mo@centralbooks.com
In North America: International Specialized Book Services, e-mail: orders@isbs.com
In Germany: LIT Verlag Fresnostr. 2, D-48159 Münster
Tel. +49 (0) 2 51-620 32 22, Fax +49 (0) 2 51-922 60 99, e-mail: vertrieb@lit-verlag.de
In Austria: Medienlogistik Pichler-ÖBZ, e-mail: mlo@medien-logistik.at
e-books are available at www.litwebshop.de

CONTENTS

MAP OF THE RESEARCH AREA (Source: www.google.com/maps

PROLOGUE

This book did not even exist as an idea in my mind one year ago. Whilst conducting field research in the broader Konitsa area, this time in the context of the THALES[1] research programme of the University of Ioannina, entitled *Nature conservation through religion: The sacred forests of Epirus*, I realised that, beyond the specific object of the study (the forests protected by religious practices), there are other related topics which have not been given their due in scientific research. Speaking to people in the village about the trees, the coppices and forests, which are protected in various ways and for a variety of reasons, I "discovered" that aside from the dedicated, excommunicated, sacred etc. trees and forests, which really are protected by religious practices -fundamentally folk ones which have been adopted by the local church and ministry- there are other more important productive practices which protect clumps of trees. They do this not for the protection of the settlements, as with the "sacred" ones, but for the very survival of the community, in which these trees, the *kladera*, play an important role as winter fodder for the animals.

[1] The present research has been co-funded by the European Union (European Social Fund - EST) and by national resources via the Operational Programme "Education and Lifelong Learning" of the National Strategic Reference Framework (NSRF) - Funded Research Project: THALES. Investment in society of knowledge via the European Social Fund.

Gradually focusing my research interest on this topic, therefore, I realised that the *kladera* do not merely constitute a very important productive practice, but a kind of social phenomenon, on the basis of which one can study the system of the local economy in a given, long-lasting historical period. The *kladero* represents the distillation of the combination of agriculture and animal breeding as well as of the whole relationship between local society and the natural environment. It gives us the capacity to penetrate the secrets of the community's survival strategies and through these the very process of the appropriation of nature, a process which refers to the concept of culture itself, in the holistic sense of the term. Consequently, the *kladero* is a means to study the economic, social and generally cultural foundation of the community. Moreover, this specific process of the appropriation of nature, which could be characterised "experiential sustainability", is linked to a particular kind of social egalitarianism. This renders the whole object not simply of specific scientific interest but also highly pertinent in a time of general crisis in our society.

We could say that this phenomenon prevails in all the agro-pastoral communities found in the "oak zone" and is imprinted on their cultural landscape, which is characterised by clumps of trees, mainly oaks, in a specific spatial arrangement and with particular morphological characteristics. These are owed to their periodic pruning, in order to use the dried branches for feeding domestic animals during the winter. We find this in all the villages of this zone in the Konitsa region. It is absent essentially only from the Alpine zone, where transhumant animal breeding prevails. In the villages known as *Mastorochoria* (Craft-villages), which make up the basic population of the region, the basis of the economy is a combination of agriculture and domestic animal breeding, out of which arises the turn to technical specialisation at a specific historical juncture.

Peklari (now Pigi) belongs to this group of villages. Why this one and not another? My second home has been Konitsa for the last fifteen years and more, and I had the opportunity in my neighbourhood - which took its name from the settlement of a number of inhabitants of Peklari and is called *Peklaritika* - to meet and associate with many of them. Thus, informally and without them realising (often also without me realising), I carried out research by discussing with them various topics of their village. The village itself is only seven kilometres from Konitsa and thus, each time I wanted to go for a short trip, by some twist of fate the road took me there. When, therefore, I had to decide on my example for the case study, I chose Peklari without a second thought.

From this position I would like to thank all the villagers who helped me in one way or another (often without realising it). I would particularly like to thank, however, Antonis and Lefko Tefou, my dear neighbours and regular interlocutors, Nikos Kefalas, former secretary of the community, Galateia Vourdouka, Pavlos Propodis, the former and current presidents Panagiotis Choupsias, Christos Kontos, Ioannis and his son Vassilis Spanos, Apostolos Zotos and all those who responded positively to my proposal and spoke with me on the relevant topics.

Warm thanks are also due to my colleagues Kalliopi Stara and Rigas Tsiakiris for our creative collaboration and their help in general, to Joshua Barley for the translation and Thodoris Kouros for the editing.

Finally, I would like to thank Dr W. Hopf, who willingly agreed to include the book in his publications.

As the book was coming to an end, my father passed away. By his actions he taught me something without which neither this book nor my other books would exist: To carry out my work with love and enthusiasm.

INTRODUCTION

NATURE AND CULTURE

The nature-culture dichotomy has left its mark on anthropological debate since the very beginnings of the scientific discipline. Even today, in a way, it occupies an important position in various discussions on a broad range of topics. The same can be said of the environment-society dichotomy, which in one way or another appears again and again in various contexts of sociological and environmental narratives.

Oddly enough, these dichotomies are reproduced even in post-modern contexts, essentially perpetuating a conception of culture as a reality external to nature, and vice versa. Culture, whether as a product of the appropriation of nature by human society or as a means of mankind's adaptation to its environment, remains a distinct entity; nature, on the other hand, continues to be portrayed as something external, an objective reality "somewhere out there", to be made into an object of use, management, exploitation etc. in one way or another.

It seems to be somewhat difficult to free ourselves from this deep-rooted dichotomous idea, which is found in the very foundations of western thought since the beginning of modernity. We could perhaps also claim that the same dichotomy is to be found in the roots of the discipline of Ecology itself. The objectification of the environment cuts it off from human society and experience in a clearly positivist way. In any case, the complete distinction between society and environment seems to be a product of the fallacy of the western intellectual tradition.[2]

On the level of the social sciences, this dialogue on the relationship between society and environment (societe/milieu) is as old as the fields of Sociology and Human Geography themselves. Moreover, the dispute between Durkheim and Ratzel is well known, as to whether the natural environment determines society and culture, or vice versa.[3] This question is, in one way or another, still present in contemporary debate about the environment, and by its presence thus demonstrates how the dichotomy which we are referring to is reproduced. In theoretical terms, the first viewpoint has been expressed and maintained by environmental determinism, and the second by cultural determinism.[4] We should note, however, that even in the context of cultural determinism, which gives priority to culture while simultaneously adopting a more dialectic approach to the relationship between nature and culture, the dichotomy is reproduced.

---

[2] See B. Latour, *We have never been modern,* Harvester/Wheatsheaf, New York, 1993 and *The politics of nature: How to bring the sciences into democracy,* Cambridge Mass., 2004 (1st ed. in French, 1999). For a historical approach to the topic, see V. Seirinidou, "Οι ιστορικοί στη φύση. Μια εισαγωγή στην περιβαλλοντική ιστορία" ("Historians in nature. An introduction to environmental history"), *Istorika,* 51, 2009, pp. 275-297.

[3] See K. Milton, *Environmentalism and Cultural Theory,* Routledge, London, 1996.

[4] See K. Milton, K., *op. cit.*, K. Eder, *The social construction of nature,* Sage, London, 1996 and E. Hirsch - M. O'Hanlon, *The Anthropology of Landscape,* Clarendon, Oxford, 1995.

The currently prevailing view in Social Anthropology tends to be that of the social and cultural construction of the natural environment. This does not mean, however, that all the theoretical and methodological problems that one faces when called to examine relevant issues have been solved. We must still stress the fact that the various approaches to the "nature-culture" and "environment-society" relationship have left several question marks, even in the field of Social Anthropology. These are related to the very notion of culture, which has received criticism not merely in the way in which we have encountered above - as something outside nature, as a means of adapting to it or in some cases as a result of the appropriation of nature by man - but since 1980 it has been seriously brought into question as a flawed analytical tool in the rapidly developing field of cultural studies.[5] In any case, the two entities appear more or less as separate phenomena, which relate to each other in one way or another, interact with each other etc. In recent years, moreover, this has fuelled new critical approaches both in the new branch of Ecological Anthropology and to those of Human and Cultural Ecology.[6]

These critiques essentially concentrate on the reproduction of the dichotomy, and the most radical even suggest a spiritualistic version of ecology, a kind of animism in which, among other things, nature and culture are presented as one entity[7].

---

[5] See L. Abu-Lughod, "Writing against culture", in R. Fox (ed.), *Recapturing anthropology: Working in the present*, Santa Fe, 1991, pp. 137-162.
[6] See K. Milton, *op. cit.*, and E. Croll - D. Parkin (eds.), *Bush base: Forest farm. Culture, environment and development*, Routledge, London, 1992.
[7] See E. Croll -D. Parkin, *op. cit.*

Of course, to support this kind of approach empirical examples are used from non-Western societies, where the people consider themselves an integral part of their natural environment and the elements of their environment are treated as animate beings, as an extension of human existence. There the natural environment is not considered something external to man, something to be exploited, negotiated with, studied etc. It is considered part of the social and cultural state of affairs, usually sacred - just like social institutions - and inextricably interwoven with the myths and rituals which maintain and reproduce society. It is a component of ritual and religious practices in general, which are of vital importance for social reproduction, and an integral part of the material and symbolic systems and processes which constitute and are constituted by what we call culture.

It is not my intention to enter into a thorough discussion of all this extremely complex issue, but I consider it essential to my topic to reflect on some of its fundamental aspects and to decide on an interdisciplinary basis which theoretical approach, which methodology and which conceptual tools I should employ in order to deal with the topic.

A fundamental theoretical view that I accept, therefore, is that "nature" is not a timeless essence, external to human society and culture. It is constructed, rather, through meaning-producing social relationships, just like all the instances of what we call "reality". Societies invest with meaning all the material conditions of their existence by producing symbolic systems, through which they appropriate and communicate with what is called "environment".

This process, which should be understood in historical and dialectical terms, comprises what we call "culture".

THE BROADER CONTEXT

ECOLOGY AND HISTORY

Space, time, landscape

Moving on from the theoretical level to more specific theories on the meaning of place and time - the fundamental components of social and cultural "reality" - on the same theoretical basis as that of "constructivism"[8], I could maintain that the two categories, although in principle "natural", from a social and cultural point of view are formed socially, which means historically. People appropriate space and time through specific social and cultural systems and turn them into cultural categories, transforming them in accordance with the prevalent historical conditions. This happens in historical terms, i.e. on the basis of the relationships of production and reproduction of the material and symbolic conditions of the life of a society, which change in time. On the basis of this dialectical way of thinking we should speak of a mutually determined process, i.e. a process whereby the culturally-formed categories of space and time simultaneously play their own role in the formation of culture.

Let us now move on, however, to the subject of landscape, which essentially imprints the historical process of the transfor-

---

[8] J. Berger - Th. Luckmann, *The social construction of reality,* Allen Lane, London, 1967.

mation of space into place through the workings of culture. Ethnographic descriptions provide from the beginning particular narratives on the places and sites in question, and they demonstrate the way in which places obtain their morphological characteristics through productive, social and ritual practices. What we call "landscape" for the indigenous people is not a chance assemblage of natural elements but a framework structured by their history and collective myths, a place inextricably interwoven with their social existence (Hirch 1995:1-30).

The view that culture transforms the natural environment into a cultural landscape is commonplace in sciences of space today, but the discussion has progressed through dialectical approaches to more "processual" points of view.[9] This means that landscape today is treated more as a process and less as an object. Moreover, another group of anthropologists and geographers have contributed to this dialogue by introducing the concept of "dwelling", used first by T. Ingold.[10] The usefulness of this concept lies in the fact that it puts forward the idea of the formation of places and landscapes through human action ("praxis"). Human praxis creates places with meaning. The appropriation of the land through cultivation or other productive uses, the knowledge of space and place as a product of labour, technology and the productive process make up what Ingold

---

[9] See T. Ingold, "Culture and the perception of the environment", in E. Croll - D. Perkin, *op. cit.* pp. 39-56, E. Hirsch - M. O'Hanlon, *op. cit.* and S. M. Low - D. Lawrence-Zuniga, "Locating culture", in S.M. Low - D. Lawrence-Zuniga (eds.) *The anthropology of space and place,* Blackwell, London, 2003, pp. 1-47

[10] See T. Ingold, *The perception of the environment,* Routledge, London, 2001.

calls "taskscapes". I believe that this term can prove highly useful in this study.

The mountainous area of the Pindus

Progressing now onto the mountainous area and landscape of the Pindus, in which my case study is located, we must above all deconstruct a myth that prevails in the rhetoric and representation of mountains even in scientific debate. It is frequently supposed that mountains represent archetypal natural landscapes, which have only recently been influenced by human activity. Somehow, particular narratives on the conservation of the environment reproduce the view that natural landscapes are good and cultural ones not, since by definition human intervention in nature damages it. That is why in various environmental conservation programmes, human presence is something which must be minimised or eliminated. This is combined, furthermore, with new approaches to mountainous land that gives priority to its environmental and aesthetic value and not to its productive uses. This is also related to the whole process of the commercialisation of nature in the context of modernity and post-modernity.

There is also a belief that mountains are distant, hostile and difficult for human adaptation and because of this people flee there only in difficult times, for example in periods of demographic pressure or politically intolerable living conditions in the plains. A good example is the prevalent national narrative in Greece on the flight of the Greek population to the mountains due to Ottoman occupation. In these contexts the mountains have transformed into symbols of freedom and national resistance.

In fact, mountain landscapes are just as anthropogenic as all the landscapes that have been shaped through historical human presence[11]. We should not study how much they resemble ideal natural environments in the context of the continuum nature/culture, but trace the historicity of the human presence in the context of the broader political economy, i.e. placing the local historically-shaped modes of production in the broader political-economic systems of which they make up a part. From this perspective the critical parameter is not bound up with the above continuum but with the dominant mode of production. On this basis, if we want to think in terms of some continuum or conceptual model, we should place at the centre of the discussion the opposition defined by two poles: on the one hand the modes of production which are based on use values, and on the other those based on exchange values. This focus would also lead us to another conceptual tool, that of *transition*, since the "forest landscapes" with which we are concerned were formed in the pre-industrial era and in the context of local systems characterised by self-sufficiency and the production of use values to a large extent. The transition to modernity entailed the gradual dominance of exchange values and the commercialisation of all aspects of life and, of course, also of natural resources. *Transition* as a concept by definition prescribes dynamic approaches and an emphasis on dialectic and historicity. The understanding of local systems presupposes a grasp of local knowledge, as well as the adoption of local categories and ways of thinking. For example, in local

---

[11] A.T. Grove - O. Rackham, *The nature of Mediterranean Europe. An ecological history*, U.P., Yale, 2001, McNeil, J.R., *The mountains of the Mediterranean world*, U.P., Cambridge, 1992.

societies the abstract concepts of nature or culture do not exist. People talk about specific objects and specific practices. It is on this basis that they apprehend and experience the space, which is transformed into place in the same way. The notion of *practice* could also be a useful tool which would free us from dichotomous approaches of every kind, as it was invented by Bourdieu precisely to overcome the difficulties regarding the definition in deterministic terms of the relationship between structure and agency.[12] In other words, Bourdieu puts forward the idea that social practice activates the sense of space. More than anything else, this brings us close to ethno-ecology, a relatively recently-formed field which is developing at the crossroads between Anthropology and Ecology and gives priority to indigenous knowledge and indigenous cosmologies[13].

Ecology, history and political economy in the Pindus

Let us attempt to see, therefore, what the situation is in the mountainous area of the Pindus with regard to the appropriation of the natural environment by local communities during the historical period in which they were given the shape we know today, and when the corresponding folk culture developed. This period is identified with that of Ottoman rule.

The mountain ecosystems of the Pindus were formed within specific and historically-defined contexts of a dialogue between local communities and their natural environment. This dialogue essentially consists of the appropriation of the natural environment by local societies based on specific social rationale, from which in

[12] Bourdieu P., *Outline of a theory of practice,* U.P., Cambridge, 1977, p. 214.
[13] See K. Milton, *op. cit.*, pp. 49-59.

turn practices arise, always in historical terms, i.e. in the context of specific modes of production and political organisation which characterise the broader entities of which the local societies are part. Thus, natural space is transformed into an anthropogenic landscape, imprinting the presence through time of human activity in general but also more specific aspects of the economy, social structures and cultural expression.

The environment represents a natural framework that prescribes specific uses and can limit the process of appropriation or exploitation of natural resources, depending on technological development and the more general social rationale. The broader framework of the relationship between local society and its natural environment is defined by the historical conditions and circumstances. Usually, the political context proves more decisive than the environment itself, since the management of natural resources and the corresponding productive relationships arise through the administrative and broader political integration of local societies in larger state formations. A typical example are the mountain communities of the Pindus themselves at their peak, i.e. in the last centuries of Ottoman rule. It is well known that the bestowal of the privilege of self-government and relative autonomy on these communities was not an internal contradiction in the Ottoman system but part of its conquering strategies[14]. What occurred, therefore, cannot be explained except in the context of these strategies as well

---

[14] See A. Vakalopoulos, *Ιστορία του Νέου Ελληνισμού* (*History of Modern Hellenism*), vol. 1., Thessaloniki, 1961 and G.D. Kontogiorgis, *Κοινωνική δυναμική και πολιτική αυτοδιοίκηση. Οι ελληνικές κοινότητες της τουρκοκρατίας* (*Social dynamics and political self-rule: Greek communities under Ottoman Rule*), Nea Synora, A. Livanis, Athens, 1982.

as the incorporation of local societies into the broader structures. Self-government enabled the local populations to manage the available natural resources with relative autonomy and of course to have the responsibility for their management. Moreover, the wider context enabled technical specialisation or exodus of the population or both at once, at times of economic difficulty and demographic deadlock. In this way, the local systems have safety valves and there is always the possibility of reducing pressure on the finite natural resources and ultimately of the survival both of the local communities and of the local ecosystems.

The significance of the broader political context for the formation, transformation and disintegration of the mountain systems, as well as the value of the concept of historicity in interpreting the above, is revealed by the developments in the mountain region in question over the last century. The mountain-plain complementarity has, over the twentieth century, undergone fundamental changes, owing precisely to the new orientation of the peasant economy and society in the context of new political conditions. The collapse in the post-war period of the once flourishing (economically, politically and culturally) mountain region is the most eloquent piece of evidence of the historicity of mountain ecosystems in relation to the societies that they sustain, since it is owed to very specific historical factors, as well as to very specific political choices, which overturned the existing equilibrium and transferred the centre of gravity from the mountains to the plains.

Ecological zones and productive processes

Henceforth we will turn our attention to the practices of the management of natural resources in this mountain region, examining the process of its formation as well as transformation in time.

The primary productive activities of agriculture and animal breeding represent the foundation for the appropriation of the natural environment in an initial phase of history, complemented by the secondary occupations of woodcutting, hunting, gathering etc. The complementarity between agriculture and animal breeding varies depending on the geomorphology and altitude. Thus, in very mountainous communities, agriculture is limited to the presence of small gardens, and animal breeding is transhumant. Pastoralists are provided with the necessary agricultural products in the plains where they spend the winter, creating reciprocal relationships with the farmers.

This variation concerning pastoral communities is not the only one that characterises the wider region. We can, however, begin with this one to refer to the diversity of the productive, social and cultural systems of the area, which shape an interesting cultural ecology. For example, there is a very interesting ethnic division of productive activities, a specialisation of ethnic groups, which has determined to a great extent their particular characteristics.

In the high zones, in what we call *alpine* landscape, historically speaking two ethnic groups predominate: the Sarakatsans and the Vlachs. We are speaking of purely or fundamentally transhumant pastoral communities, whose life and culture are inextricably interwoven with the high mountains, which they manage with very specific methods, established by custom and based on particular productive formations (*tselingato*, family flock etc.).

Thus, this ecological zone is transformed into a cultural landscape bearing the stamp of the groups which collectively appropriate it, establishing it simultaneously as a symbol of their identity. The management of the pastureland, in conjunction with the use of water and forest, shape a specific and relatively recognisable landscape, as the result of a particular and historically-defined intervention in and appropriation of nature. This is a process with its own dynamics through time, directed by the dialectical relationship itself between man and nature in its historical dimension.

In these communities, in these ethnic groups, other complementary specialisations arise via specific historical processes. These are usually within the framework of the same domestic group, which is normally a large extended family. It is a process which also expresses the groups' strategies of survival when they reach their economic and demographic limits, as well as leading many of them in time to transformation.

In particular among the Vlachs, and specifically from the 17th century onwards, the shift to commercial activities, whether through transport (*kiratzides* - mule-drivers) or the development of domestic crafts (weaving, gold and silverwork etc.), meant the transition from self-sufficiency to commercialisation of the economy. This, combined further with mobility and the new contacts and functions which all of that entailed, gradually led local societies to an economic and cultural transformation, which reached its peak in the 19th century. Typical examples were Metsovo, Syrrako, Nymfaio and other mountain communities of Northern Greece[15].

For the Sarakatsans the same cannot be said, since this group remained until recently more "faithful" to their pastoral past and historically did not develop their own villages, but used pastureland of other communities, in which they were not integrated. They preserved their own separate way of life in sheepfolds outside settlements, and in the pastureland along with their flocks.[16]

The lower zone, on the other hand - the zone where oak trees typically predominate ("oak zone") - which is also the zone of permanent habitation, i.e. the area where most mountain settlements have developed historically, reaches around 1000 metres above sea level. Here the mixed system of agriculture-animal breeding developed, in which the complementarity of these two productive activities operates not simply in the framework of the same community but also of the same domestic group. Each household typically has a smallholding, which is divided into small pieces of land in various parts of the community area, and a small number of animals that graze by day in the communal pastureland with the others of the

---

[15] See V. Rokou, *Ορεινές κοινωνίες κατά την περίοδο της οθωμανικής κυριαρχίας στα Βαλκάνια. Το Μέτσοβο της κτηνοτροφίας από τον 17ο έως τον 20ό αιώνα* (*Mountain societies during the period of Ottoman rule in the Balkans. Pastoralist Metsovo from the 17th to 20th century*), Erodios, Thessaloniki, 2007 and T. Katsougiannis, *Περί των Βλάχων των ελληνικών χωρών* (*On the Vlachs of Greek lands*), IMHA, Thessaloniki 1966.

[16] *See J. Campbell, Honour, family and patronage, Oxford U.P., 1964, A. Hatzimichali, Σαρακατσάνοι (Sarakatsans), vol.1-2, Athens, 1957 and V. Dalkavoukis, Η πένα και η γκλίτσα. Εθνοτική και εθνοτοπική ταυτότητα στο Ζαγόρι τον 20ο αιώνα (The pen and the shepherd's crook: Ethnic and ethno-local identity in the Zagori in the 20th century, Odysseas, Athens, 2005.*

village in one or more flocks. They are watched by hired shepherds, and in the evening return home to their stables.

Agriculture is characterised by mixed farming, a fact which is linked to the scattered nature of the landed property, since different crops require different soil, altitude, location etc. Thus, each household can have fields with cereals, a vineyard, gardens, fruit trees etc. It should be noted here that in order to maximise the yield of the sloping terrain, the well-known terraces were devised, which took on particular ecological significance (retention of soil, concentration of reptiles etc.) and give the mountain landscape its aesthetic character.

The whole system ensures the possibility of self-sufficiency as well as security through the alternative possibilities of production, as the household does not depend on just one crop. There is also the capacity for crop rotation and letting land lie fallow. If we add to this the presence of *kladera*, i.e. coppices used for pruning (branches that are stored in various ways as fodder for animals in the winter[17], along with protected coppices, usually *vakoufika* - the property of a monastery), as well as the trees or bushes of the bank that make up the natural boundaries of the properties, we have an image of a characteristic landscape with a great variety of species, a

---

[17] See P. Halstead, "Ask the fellows who lop the hay: Leaf-fodder in the mountains of Northwest Greece", *Rural History*, 9 (1998), 2, pp. 211-234. Also, E. Karamanes, *Οργάνωση του χώρου, τεχνικές και τοπική κοινότητα στα Κοπατσαροχώρια των Γρεβενών* (*Spatial organisation, techniques and local community in the* Kopatsarochoria *of Grevena*), Academy of Athens: KEEL, Athens, 2012, pp. 210-216.

landscape that corresponds to a very durable anthropogenic ecosystem. It really is a model of "anthropogenic ecodynamics", which is understood of course on the basis of the wider historical context as well as regional and inter-regional equilibria of small-scale productive and social systems. Local societies adapt to the elements of the natural environment on which they depend but they also adapt it to their needs in such a way as to ensure that the available resources do not run out. Moreover, in time, ways out of economic and demographic difficulties are found, so that the equilibrium in local systems is not put at risk. Technical specialisation, mobility or even migration provide such solutions.

Regarding the complementarity between agriculture and animal breeding, we should stress, apart from its economic dimension, also its ecological one. The phenomenon of natural fertilisation of fields by the flocks is well known, for example. It is consciously sought by the community, for during the warm months - according to local tradition - the community's flocks sleep in turn in different fields of the villagers, in order to "manure" them. The fields are also fertilised naturally by the flocks when they are pastured after the harvest until they are ploughed again for the new period of cultivation[18]. The storage of hay also has a clear role, which is cut from the fields and used as fodder for animals in the winter to prevent overgrazing. This can also be avoided by pasturing flocks in the fields after the harvest.

The position of settlements, their orientation as well as their structure itself, meets the total needs of the communities in relation

---

[18] See D. Loukopoulos, *Ποιμενικά της Ρούμελης* (*Pastoral Roumeli*), I. Sideris, Athens, 1930.

to their productive activities, climate conditions, management of natural resources (water, forest, land for cultivation etc.), the broader system of spatial organisation, transportation and communication, safety conditions etc.

Settlements are usually found in the geometric centre of the community area, so that access to all points of it is possible with pre-industrial technology. In the cases where communities have arable land far from the settlement, such that return to the village in the evening is impossible, we observe the development of a second rudimentary settlement with huts and storehouses, where the inhabitants stay overnight on the days of intense farm labour. The crop is also stored here. These settlements are usually called *Kalyvia* (Huts) and it is telling that in many cases during the post-war era, in which a more general tendency of population movement from the mountains to the plains is observable, new villages are built in places of old huts, as these places are usually closer to the nearby highways. A typical example is the well-known village of Kalpaki in Epirus, which was created in the 1950s mainly by inhabitants of the mountain villages of Elafotopos, and Ano and Kato Soudena in the Zagori (among them were also Sarakatsans who had already been accepted into these communities), in the place where previously they had their huts and fields[19].

Also in this category of communities, from one point in time onwards, typically after the 17th century, we observe the phenomenon of technical specialisation as a solution to the demographic

---

[19] See V. Nitsiakos - M. Arapoglou - K. Karanatsis, *Νομός Ιωαννίνων. Σύγχρονη πολιτισμική γεωγραφία* (*Prefecture of Ioannina: Contemporary cultural geography*), Ioannina Prefecture Government, Ioannina, 1998.

and economic difficulties that were created. It is a "way out", which also, of course, means exodus, mainly a seasonal one of the male population, but later also permanent, i.e. settlement in other places. This happens to a great extent when the plains begin to be evacuated by the Ottoman landowners as well as when new arable areas are created by the draining of bogs and the more general changes in the agricultural economy, favouring the development of farming at the expense of animal breeding. These phenomena began to appear from the time of Independence and reached their pinnacle in the first decades of the 20th century with the Agrarian Reform[20].

Regarding technical specialisation, which usually means seasonal migration of the male population, we should note that the practice of crafts in Greece during Ottoman rule is a phenomenon that developed fundamentally in the mountain regions, where entire villages or clusters of villages specialised in specific crafts: builders, painters-icon painters, carpenters-woodcarvers, tailors, coopers, coal dealers etc. In this way communities can reproduce themselves, avoiding the exhaustion of the natural resources available to them and giving households the possibility of additional income. This, of course, leads to a new division of labour by gender, since with the specialisation and exodus of men, the farming and animal breeding occupations remain mainly in the hands of the women. The exodus for commerce, on the other hand, when it happens, leads to deeper transformations, often to economic upsurge as

---

[20] See K. Vergopoulos, *Το αγροτικό ζήτημα στην Ελλάδα* (*The agricultural question in Greece*), Exantas, Athens, 1975.

well as social prosperity and cultural flourishing. The example of the villages of the Zagori speaks for itself.

PEKLARI (PIGI)

The place and the people, its nature and society in their historical context

Peklari (Pigi) is part of the cultural unity of the Mastorochoria in the region of Konitsa, a group of villages located in the valley of the Sarantaporos, a tributary of the Aoos, characterised ecologically by the oak zone, which we described above (see map) [21]

The village is situated 7 kilometres from Konitsa, next to the Konitsa-Distrato road, which also leads to Grevena via Vasilitsa (Smolika). It is a mountain village built at an altitude of 750 m. on the fringes of a forested mountain range, located in the south-west approaches of the Smolika mountain group and north-east of Konitsa. More specifically, it lies on the slopes of this mountain range with local peaks from South to North of Topolitsa (1682 m.), Kolokythia (2022 m.), and Lolos (1851m). Understandably, the gradient of the terrain above the settlement and up to the peak of the mountain is very steep, but it also has many ridges and steep slopes with deep crevices. This makes the whole area inaccessible. The terrain is more even in the hilly formations near the village, where in the past the crops were grown.

---

[21] See V. Nitsiakos (ed.), *Η Κόνιτσα και τα χωριά της. Πολιτισμού ανατομή* (*Konitsa and its villages: An Anatomy of Culture*), Prefecture of Ioannina - Epirus A.E., Ioannina, 2008, pp.120-143.

These slopes are also characterised by the presence of springs and streams which flow through them and meet near the village, forming the Topolitsa (Lakkos) watercourse. They are directed via Klisoura to the outskirts of the plain of Konitsa (at Boussi) and ultimately flow into the Aoos river. Despite the steep incline of the terrain, the streams are not torrential except during the winter. This is because the drainage basin is covered by forest, which developed mainly after the abandonment of agriculture and animal breeding and the general decline in population of the village after WWII and particularly after the 1970s. The large number of gullies and streams in parallel arrangement and with alternating waterfalls draw material from the disintegration of limestone and deposit it in the lower part, where the crops were. This creates deep and productive land. The two main streams, Kolokythia and Motsiali (locally known as Lakkos and Potamos), keep their water throughout the year, as they are fed by the abundant springs in the forest.

The presence of the forest is dominant on the slopes and peaks around the village, with the pines and firs occupying the greatest area and extending more and more to the areas near the village, which were for crops until recently. Thus, they tend to dominate the lower slopes and plateaus, where along with the fields there used to be oak trees used for pruning, the so-called *kladera*. At the highest altitudes the Bosnian pine predominates, which grows at around 1400 m. to 2000 m. and at its lowest points merges with the black pine and the fir. In the pine and fir forest we sporadically find deciduous trees - on their own or in small clusters - such as species of oak, cedar, maple, ash, hornbeam, dogwoods etc. Climbing ivy also has a significant presence, as well as mistletoe, semi-parasitical on forest trees. These are elements of the flora that are important for domestic livestock. On the banks of the streams, hydrophilic trees such as planes and willows are in evidence.

Regarding the dynamic of the forest and of the "plant communities", one easily observes that, as farming and animal breeding activities are abandoned, the black pine tends to spread into the open areas, pushing aside the existing broad-leaved trees, and the fir expands in the pine forest, developing a kind of "competition".

The expansion of the forest into the former fields, the *kladera* and the pastureland creates an image of the recovery of nature on the one hand, and desolation on the other. The marks of human presence - both productive and cultural more generally - are covered up by vegetation; roads and paths close up; the formerly tamed and humanised space grows wild.

Now only one part of the former shepherds' pastureland is used, and only during the summer, by the two flocks of sheep and goats that spend the winter in a place on the outskirts of the plain of Konitsa quite near the town known as Boussi (small-scale transhumance). These flocks now use the broad expanse of Prosilio, a place near the village that used to be arable land and *kladera*. It was also used as pastureland.

In this ecological framework, there is a humid continental climate with cold winters and cool summers. The winter period is characterised by frequent frosts. Rainfall in the region is very common (about 1600mm per year), with uneven distribution between seasons. The summer dry season is short, and during the other months of the cold season rain is abundant and long-lasting. Frosts and snowfall are usual during the winter period, particularly in the more mountainous areas.

The village is built in four districts: Upper *machalas* (quarter), Lower *machalas* and Outer *machalas* (Mantzaioi and Spanaioi). Between the Upper and Lower *machalas* is the square, while the Outer *machalas* is separated from the others by the stream. The built area is located at the foot of the mountain and the area around it is characterised by former arable land, now abandoned, that is becoming forest at a rapid rate. Below the village and along the main stream are fertile, irrigated fields, on which the arable production in the past was based to a large extent. North of the village, at Prosilio, are most of the village's *kladera*, as well as what is now an important stretch of pastureland. Generally speaking the forest, fields (now abandoned), pastureland and *kladera* make up the "environment" of the community, which is totally anthropogenic and bears the stamp of appropriation by the inhabitants for production. To understand and explain it, therefore, we must look historically at the development of productive processes and relationships, and their successive impact on the place.

According to the few historical sources at our disposal, and to local oral tradition, today's community is made up of families who previously inhabited settlements in Plaka and Boussi, near today's national road between Ioannina and Kozani, after the bridge of Topolitsa as you leave Konitsa heading for the Mastorochoria. According to the sources, Peklari seems to have already been a *tsiftlik* (privately-owned estate) by 1850. It was probably made such by Ali Pasha (1750-1822), while previously it was a *kefalochori*, i.e. self-governed community. It remained a *tsiftlik* until around 1870, when it was bought out by the inhabitants and became "free" again[22]. It is characteristic that former inhabitants of Konitsa remembered Russit Bey, the "Turko-konitsiote" as the last owner of the *tsiftlik*. Shortly before the buying out of the village, the *tsiftlik* of Boussi seems to have been bought out by the Kitsos and Spanos families[23], who own the plot of land up to today.

Regarding population, Peklari appears to have had 322 inhabitants in the census of 1846 and 612 in that of 1874[24]. Twenty years later, in 1894, it is presented as having 700 inhabitants (*Foni tis Ipirou*, 11-2-1894). From its integration into the Greek state in 1913 onwards, the demographic picture of the community is reflected in the respective censuses: 1913:282, 1920:351, 1928:339, 1940:379, 1951:362, 1961:398, 1971:225, 1981:191, 1991: 199.

---

22 See C. Goutos, *Η επαρχία Κόνιτσας και η Μόλιστα επί τουρκοκρατίας* (*The Konitsa district and Molista under Ottoman rule*), Athens, 2003. pp. 28-40.

23 See A. Efthymiou, "Η Πηγή (Πεκλάρι)" ("Pigi (Peklari)"), *Konitsa*, 9, 1963, pp. 8-9.

24 See P. Aravantinos, *Χρονογραφία της Ηπείρου* (*Chronicle of Epirus*), vol. 2, Athens, 1856, pp. 339-341, 367 and M. Kokolakis, *Το ύστερο Γιαννιώτικο πασαλίκι. Χώρος, διοίκηση και πληθυσμός στην Τουρκοκρατούμενη Ήπειρο (1820-1913)* (*The last* pashalik *of Yannina: Place, administration, and population in Ottoman Epirus*), PhD thesis, Athens, 1993, p. 324.

Population changes in Peklari (150 years)

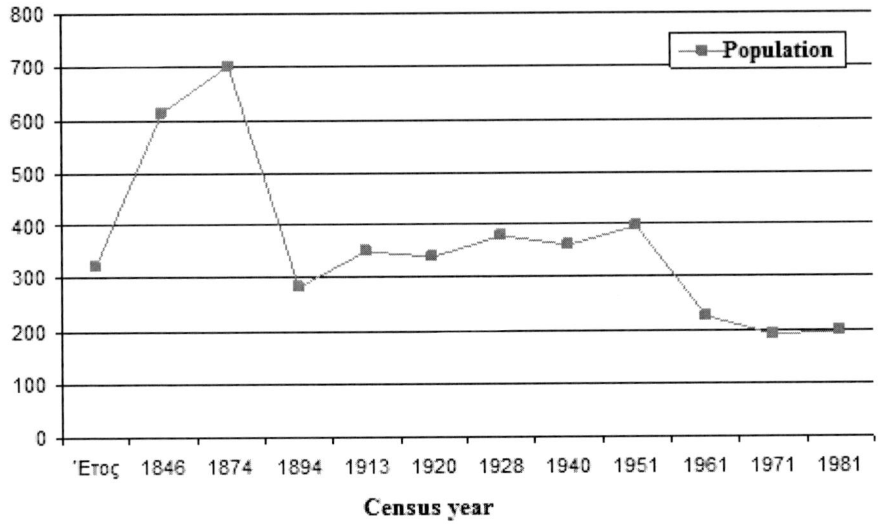

The above data comes from the National Statistical Service and we do not know to what degree they reflect reality, given the seasonal absence of the male population. Over the last decades the population data from censuses is fictitious, since the practice has prevailed of people living elsewhere (particularly in the urban centres) going to the village to register in the census. In any case, it is clear that population decline was approaching the point of abandonment in the 1980s, a situation which worsened in the following decades. It is telling that in 1975 the active members of the Forest Association of the Community numbered just 13 (source: Community Archive). Today there are 32 permanent inhabitants, the vast majority elderly. Essentially, one couple is below 60, and the husband works in

Konitsa. There is no one, therefore, who lives in the village permanently and works in agriculture or animal breeding. Only a few gardens are cultivated, and a small number of domestic goats are kept. The animal breeders reside in Boussi and Konitsa and go up to the village pastureland in the summer, where they have sheepfolds.

In the 1970s, the community went through its final phase as a productive body, combining small-scale agriculture, domestic animal breeding, woodcutting, and the occupation of the itinerant craftsman. Since the 1980s, the population decline has reached proportions of abandonment and desolation, marking the end of a long period of community life and the start of a new era, during which the countryside becomes a place of nostalgic "return", for holidays and aesthetic consumption. Thus today the 32 permanent inhabitants can reach 150 in summer, with the addition of the summer vacationers.

The appropriation of natural resources. The productive processes and the landscape.

The natural resources of the community, as has already been made clear, are the soil, forests, trees, arable areas, pastureland and water. The borders between forest, arable areas and pastureland are not clear. On the contrary, we observe a permeation between them and a multiple usage, which is combined further with a kind of multifunctionality. For example, animals can graze in the forests, when there is no particular reason to protect them, and in the arable areas after the harvest. In the past, the arable areas could have been extended at the expense of the forest by the practices of *xerongiasma* (slashing and burning) and *trafokopima* (digging up). Over the last decades, however, with the abandonment of agriculture, the forest penetrates into the arable areas. Moreover, in the *kladera,* which used to be in the arable areas, the domestic animals were pastured after the harvest through a specific, collective management according to the grazing capacity of each stretch of land -some small, some large. Following their abandonment, however, they became common pastureland for the transhumant flocks.

What is and what is not forest

Regarding forest, it would be useful here to reflect on the conceptual definition of the term, since multiple questions arise in the treatment of this topic, precisely to do with its definition: what is and what is not forest. This becomes more important given that the present study fundamentally concerns the protection of forests of all forms, in the context of the more general management of the natural environment on a local level.

Let us begin, therefore, with the science of Forestry. According to the definition, "forest is the ecosystem in which on a favourable surface, trees, bushes and herbaceous vegetation coexist in a close social relationship. There, according to the degree of canopy cover, they create a particular environment with distinct characteristics -the dasogenic environment- in which all the plant and animal organisms create, through mutual interactions and interdependence, a distinct bio-community, the forest bio-community. Forest bio-communities do not remain constant over time, but have an internal dynamic of change towards more complex or more simple forms of organisation, depending on the internal natural processes and external influences. With the term 'forest area' we mean a forest ecosystem that is differentiated from the forest, mainly in the reduced level of canopy cover of woody or bushy vegetation."[25]

Although on a scientific level the matters are clear, and the dynamic nature of forest -and not only forest- ecosystems is defined, in the context of management and legal matters the same cannot be said. If you delve into the relevant bibliography and case law, you will be faced with a veritable maze of laws and other related documents and decisions of state agencies and services. These make clear the huge problem in the management of forests, revolving around the definition of forest, since all the decisions on its management depend upon this definition. Indicatively, it will suffice to mention a typical expression of the President of the Council of State in an article on the "thirty years war of the forests from the judicial front". He writes, "Another method of maintaining the war on forests by the government was the legislative alteration of the concept of forest. There was even a bill that entrusted the definition of forest to the decision of the Minister of Agriculture...".[26] It is not my intention to deal with this aspect, but I touch on the question because it has an impact on local communities in terms of land ownership and more specifically the change from agricultural to forest areas, which

---

[25] See P. Smyris, "Εισαγωγή: Το δασικό οικοσύστημα" ("Introduction: The forest ecosystem"), in A.H. Papageorgiou - G. Karetsos - G. Katsadorakis (ed.), *Το δάσος. Μια ολοκληρωμένη προσέγγιση* (*Forest: A comprehensive study*), WWF Greece, Athens, 2012, pp.13-15, p. 14. See also S. Dafis, *Δασική οικολογία* (*Forest ecology*), Giachoudis-Giapoulis publications, Thessaloniki, 1986, pp. 1-12.

[26] M. Dekleris, "Ο Τριακονταετής πόλεμος των δασών: το μέτωπο της Δικαιοσύνης" ("The Thirty Years' war of the forests: The judicial front"), http://www.oikipa.gr/index.php/-mainmenu-63/118-asi (6/10/2014).

come into public ownership when they are abandoned and afforested. Moreover, the whole question enables us to shed light in a number of ways on the perceptions of, engagement with and uses of the natural environment on a local level and in contrast with the central, official state. At the political and legal level, therefore, the "war" for the "uses of land" continues even today, in a particularly intense way regarding forests and pastureland, and thus the relevant definitions change depending on the respective political decisions. In a scientific context, however, the approaches and of course the relevant definitions touch more and more on local "traditional" ways of thinking about the forest as an open and dynamic ecosystem, whose borders are not clear nor are the uses strictly defined and static in space and time.

According to the most recent theories in the relevant scientific disciplines, and that of Forestry itself, ecological systems are permanently open to external influences, have no clear boundaries, and their equilibrium is dynamic even when no changes are observed. All this means that the scientific approach is not consistent with any case law or legislation on the ownership and uses of land in rural areas and, moreover, that socio-political situations usually lead to the circumvention of scientific principles. Scientifically, based on the concept of the open and dynamic character of forest ecosystems, the question of what is and is not forest cannot be defined in strict terms. In Greece particularly, where there are no "virgin" forests, but all are more or less shaped in relation to human activity (with the forest itself or with agriculture/animal breeding), the question must be faced in view of history, the political economy and local practices through time.

On the basis of this position and given the more general references to the context of the history, political economy and cultural ecology of the Pindus, let us now turn to the question of local engagement with and perceptions of the forest.

Let us begin with an extract from a very interesting text from the 1960s, which was written by a forester and concerns "forest folklore": "...the mountain villager of Epirus derives around 92% of his income each year from agriculture and animal breeding, but just 8% from forestry. This is why the mountain villager shows such indifference to the fate of the forest, which he sees either as land to be made cultivable (*xyloma*) or as pastureland, and on this account refuses to abandon nomadic or semi-domestic animal breeding and turn to forestry...".[27] The above observation is basically correct but the generalised judgement of the "indifference" of the villager to the forest is, in my view, mistaken. This will be apparent in my approach and in the data that I present below. For the time being it will suffice to say that the forest is not understood by the villager in the manner which it is understood by the state administration, the "forest" professionals and the urban population. Moreover, the various local strategies and management practices of the natural environment demonstrate that where there is need, protective measures are taken through an "experiential sustainable approach", since the villagers know full well the limits of the natural resources that belong to them, as they know that they cannot survive if they exhaust these resources. Collective decisions and customary methods of

---

[27] P. Grispos, "Δασική λαογραφία" ("Forest folklore"), *Ipeirotiki Estia* (1967), p. 527.

tree, coppice and forest protection provide the most tangible evidence of the awareness of the importance of these elements, not only for economic survival and social reproduction but also for quality of life, avoidance of dangers (such as soil erosion, which can lead to the destruction of a settlement) etc.

The word "forest" (*dasos*) itself seems to be introduced into local societies through administration and particularly through the state forestry services. From Independence onwards,[28] these took on the management of the forests and have had a highly intrusive presence in issues concerning not only the forests but more broadly the management of the natural environment, since the definition of what is and is not forest changes and becomes an object of social and political tension, as we will see below.

---

[28] Knowledge of the Ottoman regime can play an important part in understanding the issue of forests. Many topics related to the definition of forest seem to arise from it. Let us note here merely that forest during the Ottoman period, at least from the 19th century onwards, are divided into three categories: a) *orman*, public forests, b) *baltalik*, forests that were given to the inhabitants of communities for woodcutting and g) *koru*, forest in which the trees were "private". See, indicatively, P. Grispos, *Δασική ιστορία της νεωτέρας Ελλάδος. Από του ΙΕ΄αιώνος μέχρι του 1971 συγγραφείσα επί τη 150ετηρήδι της Εθνικής παλιγγενεσίας* (*A history of forests in modern Greece: From the 15th century until 1971, written on the 150th anniversary of the national regeneration*), Ministry of National Economy, Athens 1973 and A. Oikonomopoulos, *Η εξέλιξις της δασοπονίας εν τη νέα Ελλάδι. Από της απελευθερώσεως αυτής μέχρι του έτους 1940* (*The development of forestry in modern Greece. From Liberation until 1940*), University of Thessaloniki, Thessaloniki 1942.

The most common terms in local societies of Epirus - and the rest of Greece - for forest are *longos* (literally "thicket") and *ormani* or *roumani*. In oral literature the term *longos* is found most often.

Looking at the relevant linguistic and forest-folklore sources, we have concluded that there are various views on what the term *longos* precisely means. According to one view, it means a "low" forest or coppice. According to another, it is a "high" forest, analogous to the French *longue*. According to the forester P. Grispos, the term initially meant "lake" or a place flooded by water, a wet expanse, which is usually also wooded, covered by aquatic plants. In this regard he mentions the name of Mesolongi as the most characteristic. The term, he says, went on to mean "forest" - aquatic forest. We find place names such as Pefkolongos, Elatolongos, Strolongos, Kastanolongos, Oxolongos, which demonstrate how the term is extended in its meaning and ends up being used even for fruit-bearing trees. For example, during the years of Ottoman rule the olive grove of Athens was called a *longos*[29].

In any case, *longos* is not to be identified with *dasos*, in the way that it is understood from a certain point onwards, based on the intrusion of science and the state. *Longos* quintessentially refers to an area with wooded vegetation shaped by human activity (woodcutting, pruning, grazing etc.). Even the term *ormani*, which refers to a more wooded expanse, is not to be identified with the

---

[29] See P. Grispos, *op. cit.*, 19 (1970), p. 462. See also S.K. Tsitsas, *T' αγριόδεντρα του βουνού και του λόγγου* (*The wild trees of the mountain and the* longos), Centre of Environmental Education in Mouzaki, Karditsa, 2009 (1st edition 1978), in which it seems that the term *longos* is normally used for local or "traditional" references, while *dasos* is used in a modern, scientific context.

notion of *dasos*, as it is usually understood today. For example, in the Zagori *ormania* referred to properties that had *kladera* but which were simultaneously cultivated and grazed on the basis of a particular system of "sustainable" management[30]. It is also worth mentioning that many "forests" (*dasi*) in the Zagori bear the toponym *livadi* (meadow). At first sight this seems oxymoronic -how can a forest be called a meadow? A linguist has given the seemingly convincing explanation that "places known by the above toponym [*livadi*] at one time were wooded (in most instances these forests are characterised as areas of protection, in which any activity is forbidden) and at other times rich pastureland or fields. The place name designates wooded areas in the villages of Vradeto, Kalota, Lesnitsa, Manasi, Negades, Dresteniko, Petra, while in the other villages it designates pastureland... The development of the meaning from "pasture" to "forest" arises from the fact that original stretches of pastureland (which had already been called *Livadi* - Meadows) were later kept from such use for protective reasons (e.g. retention of stones, soil etc.). Thus, the places with the name *Livadi* continued to bear their original name even after the creation of forests. It should be noted that in none of the Balkan languages where the Greek word *livadi* exists as a loan word does it have the meaning of

---

[30] See V. Fanitsios, *Το δασικό ζήτημα* (*The forest question*), Athens, 1959, K. Lazaridis, *Η ατομική ιδιοκτησία στο Ζαγόρι (η μια πλευρά του δασικού μας ζητήματος)* (*Individual ownership in the Zagori (or one side of the forest question*), Ioannina, 1972. It is also telling that in a doctoral thesis on the place names of the Zagori, there is no glossary entry *dasos*, not even as a compound word. See K.E. Oikonomou, *Τοπωνυμικό της περιοχής Ζαγορίου* (*Toponyms of the Zagori region*), PhD thesis, Scientific Yearbook of the *Dodoni* Philosophy Faculty, Appendix no. 45, Ioannina, University of Ioannina, 1991.

'forest'".[31] This is not, however, completely correct, since the "forests" in question, being protected, were normally used all along as pasture and *kladera* in the context of their protection, with particular rules and prohibitions. Consequently it is not "reforestation" of former pasture (meadows), but rather a particular system of management-protection, in which we could speak about *dasolivada* – "forest-meadows", meaning the meadow area in which scattered trees, coppices or thickets of wooded vegetation grow[32].

In Greece, besides, there were never "virgin" forests. Even in the very mountainous parts, the large forests of beech, pine etc. belong to the communal areas of animal breeding communities and therefore always form part of their wider area of pastureland, in the sense that they are located lower than the mountain meadows and therefore the flocks cross them to get there (or, in other cases, they use them, e.g. on rainy days for mushrooms, on sunny days for shade). Moreover, these forests have clearings and sparse areas in

---

[31] See Oikonomou K.E., *op. cit.* p. 182.

[32] See K. Stara - R. Tsiakiris, "Τα λιβάδια που ήταν δάση. Η περίπτωση των προστατευτικών δασών του Ζαγορίου" ("The meadows that were forests: The case of the protected forests of the Zagori"), in A. Sidiropoulou, K. Mantzanas, I. Ispikoudis (eds.), *Πρακτικά 7ου Πανελληνίου Λιβαδοπονικού Συνεδρίου "Λιβαδοπονία και ποιότητα ζωής" (Proceedings of the 7th Panhellenic Rangeland Conference, "Rangeland and quality of life")*, Xanthi 14-16/10/2010, Thessaloniki, 2010, pp. 57-62. See also V. Papanastasis, "Λιβαδική αξία των δασών της βαλανιδιάς" ("Rangeland value of oak forests"), in *Δάση βαλανιδιάς: Παρελθόν, παρόν και μέλλον* (*Oak forests: Past, present and future*), Conference proceedings, T.E.I. Mesolongi - T.E.I. Lamia, Mesolongi 2002, pp. 47-52.

general which are used in many ways as pastureland, forming a vital aspect of the shepherds' organisation of space[33]. It is also well-known that in the past and until the last war, the system of *xerongiasma* was also in place in these forests. This is deforestation with the intention of cultivation, a practice recorded in the places named *Rongia*, which exist in almost all the villages of the mountain region, even in communities of transhumant Vlach pastoralists[34]. As for the

---

[33] *See V. Nitsiakos, Οι ορεινές κοινότητες της Βόρειας Πίνδου. Στον απόηχο της μακράς διάρκειας (Mountain communities of the North Pindus: In the echoes of the long durée) Plethron, Athens 1995, pp. 37-78.*

[34] For the practice of *xerongiasma* see D. Loukopoulos, *Αγροτικά της Ρούμελης* (*Agricultural Roumeli*), Athens, 1938, P. Grispos, *Δασική ιστορία της νεωτέρας Ελλάδος* (*A history of forests in modern Greece*), Ministry of National Economy, General Directorate of Forests, Athens 1973 and D.K. Psychogios, *Προίκες, φόροι, σταφίδα και ψωμί. Οικονομία και οικογένεια στην αγροτική Ελλάδα του 19ου αιώνα* (*Dowries, taxes, raisins and bread. Economy and family in agricultural Greece of the 19th century*), E.K.K.E., Athens 1995. On the toponym *Rongi* in the region of Konitsa, see C. Rembelis, *Κονιτσιώτικα* (*Konitsa matters*), "I Proodos" Association of Asimochoritans in Athens, Athens 2005 (1st edition, Epirote Society of Athens, Athens 1953). On page 274 the editor of the book N. C. Rembelis notes, "The word *rongi* is a field sown by the burning of the bushes on it (C. Souli, Ipirotika Chronika Vol. 7, p. 239). According to K. Mertzios the word is either Albanian *rogë*, meaning the relatively large distances between pines and firs, or Latin *rogus* = fire. Irrespective of whether the word came from Albanian or Latin, it is found in many villages signifying a field, or level surface coming from burning and cutting down trees...It is worth noting that in Vourbiani they use the phrase "they became *rongi*" or "they fell as *rongi*" ("they" being wheat or maize), when the ripening wheat and maize bend, break and fall to the ground as a consequence of strong wind, rain etc. The field, therefore, is apparently flattened... I believe that these metaphorical phrases clearly explain that

lower oak zone, it is self-evident that the combination of agriculture and animal breeding did not leave any margin for the development of large and thick forests, as pruning was a basic practice that aimed at the securing of fodder for the stabled animals in the winter months, since they did not move, as we shall see in detail below.

The problem of the definition of forest, which is at the heart of a long conflict on the environment more generally and has caused -and still causes- clashes between local communities and central authority, is also linked to the fact of Bavarian rule in Greece from the establishment of the Greek state. The Bavarians, based on the northern perceptions of forests, took its meaning for granted. This did not match the Greek reality. G. Maurer writes characteristically, "When we first came to Greece, everyone told us that according to the prevailing view, there were no national forests. But we found at least three. Oak and beech forests in Messenia, Evia and Roumeli. In order to preserve them, we assigned several young German foresters. Woodcutting was regulated under the supervision of the Ministry of Finance, since there was previously no control in this area."[35]

---

the word *rong*i meant the area of a forest without trees, formed by burning and cutting down of bushes and trees in it, in order to be used for cultivation. In time these cultivated pieces of land (*rongia*) were abandoned by their owners and, naturally, were reforested again. Thus today these places are forested."

[35] See G. Maurer, *Ο ελληνικός λαός* (*The Greek people*), Tolidis, Athens, 1976, p. 588. c.f. A. Kapetanios, "Η περιπέτεια του ορισμού του δάσους" ("The adventure of the definition of forest", http://dasarxeio.com/2014/06/14/605/. For a similar discussion, see also A. Oikonomou, *Φύση, τεχνολογία και κοινωνία στις ορεινές κοινότητες του Κιθαιρώνα* (*Nature, technology and society in the mountain communities of Kithairona*), Odysseas, Athens, 2007, pp. 54-60. and T. Dasoulas,

From the moment that the relevant legislation was put in place, based on the north-European perception of the forest and its protection, significant issues arose, with a serious impact on local societies, an impact which is still visible in communities and their natural environment. On the one hand, therefore, we find perceptions and use practices of "forests" for woodcutting, agriculture and animal breeding, based on local systems of production and management of natural resources, with a strong presence of human productive activity; on the other, a more "environmentalist" and protective perception of the forest as an important environmental good. The inevitable consequences were conflict, a long struggle and a tug-of-war, affecting society and state up to today. Of course, the abandonment and desolation of the mountain region has somewhat solved the social problem, but its broader dimensions have particular interest.

The "forests" of the community

The community of Pigi has "exclusive ownership and possession" in a forest, which was handed over by the state in 1930 as "protective" (article 49 of Law 4173 'On Forest Code' with the decision No.27225/11-9-1930, Order of the Administration of Epirus). Since

---

Αγροτικές κοινωνίες του ορεινού χώρου κατά την οθωμανική περίοδο. Ο γεωργικός κόσμος της χώρας Μετσόβου (18ος αι. 19ος αι.) (*Farming societies of the mountain region during the Ottoman period: The agricultural world of the land of Metsovo (18th - 19th century)*, PhD thesis, Ioannina, 2009, pp. 229-247.

then this forest, of around 2000 *stremmata*, is considered "communal", which means that the members of the community "enjoy from it the necessary amounts of useful wood and firewood, and graze their sheep and goats in the non-restricted areas by consent of the Community"[36].

In the 1975 management study of the Konitsa Forestry Authority we find,

"The owner of the forest under management is the Legal Body of the Community of Pigi (Peklari), Konitsa.

This community, in this case as a smaller, local unit of self-government in the framework of the more general development of the State, seeks the most successful handling of the economic resources.

As a body of communal benefit, it places as its main objective the considered organisation of all Forestry towards securing the greatest possible amount and best possible quality of the forest's products, in order to ensure the necessary economic resources cover on the one hand the fixed Administrative overheads - wages, carrying out projects of communal benefit etc. - and on the other hand the individual needs of the inhabitants-members of the Community in forest products.

Moreover, for the management of the forest it ensures the conditions of employment of the members of the E.D.S.E. [Forest

---

[36] See Forestry Authority of Konitsa, *Διαχειριστική μελέτη κοινοτικού δάσους Πηγής* (*Management study of the communal forest of Pigi*), Konitsa, 1975, p. 8.

Collective] of Pigi in forest work, excepting the existing possibilities of work in the adjacent Public forests.

The Community creates its annual budget from its income, which is received from the commercial renting out of its forest, and from state subsidies.

The above objective of the improvement of the economic position of the Community directs the practice of Communal Forestry towards the attainment of greater benefits from the forest in ensuring the following basic principles:

a) The conservation of the forest for its protection from influences of every kind and especially biogenic ones

b) The improvement or reduction of existing unregulated kinds of management in favour of properly regulated management".

And below,

"Primarily, the envisaged area of Pigi's forest, by its position in the village's favour is considered 'Protective', and its protective influences are numerous, both on the soil itself and on the houses below... the settlement of Pigi, situated at the foot of the communal forest receives its main protective influence... The protection provided by the forest is judged moderately satisfactory in as much as the greater part of the clumps of trees have light canopy cover and in places is of rocky composition, while at some points localised erosion can be observed, resulting in the complete absence of leaf litter. This situation is pregnant with dangers of surface, linear or furrow erosion.

It is, therefore, clear that the maintenance and expansion of the existing forest is imperative in the eroded places, for the implementation of considered and prudent management."[37]

From the above emerges the necessity of protecting the forest in question as "protective". We can conjecture that it was precisely for this reason that it was handed over by the state to the community, which was evidently interested in its protection since it guarded the settlement from floods and erosion. Its presence was generally necessary for the existence of the settlement. This forest, besides, is locally called *Kouri,* a name which is usually given to the protective forests of settlements[38]. Essentially, the state sanctions and strengthens a local practice of protection, establishing the community again as responsible for the preservation of a decisively beneficial "natural" element of the existence of the village - and not only of the village.

---

[37] See *op. cit.*, pp. 8-13.

[38] On the etymology and meaning of the term *kouri,* the discussion is open. See P. Grispos, "Το κουρί στην Ήπειρο" ("The *kouri* in Epirus"), *Ipeirotiki Estia,* May 1952, pp. 199-203 and July 1952, pp. 296-299, I. Ispikoudis, "Ιστορική και πολιτισμική θεώρηση των δασογεωργικών συστημάτων" ("A historical and cultural view of forest-agricultural systems"), *Proceedings* of Helexpo Zootechnia, Thessaloniki, 3-6 February 2005, pp. 28-40, I. Ispikoudis, M.K. Sioliou "Το πολιτισμικό τοπίο της περιοχής Πορταϊκού- Περτουλίου της Νότιας Πίνδου" ("The cultural landscape of the Portaikos - Pertouli region of the Southern Pindus"), *Geotechnika Epistimonika Themata,* 2, 15, 1, 2004, pp. 37-45, G. Maris - M. Karatasiou - K. Stara, "Το 'κουρί' στο Ζαγόρι της Ηπείρου και η σύνδεσή του με τα δασολιβαδικά οικοσυστήματα" ("The 'kouri' in the Zagori of Epirus and its link with the forest-rangeland ecosystems"), *Proceedings* of the 16th Forestry Conference. Greek Forestry Association, Thessaloniki, 2013, pp. 747-752 and Th. Dasoulas, *op. cit.*

Within this forest there are also cultivated, "privately-owned" pieces of agricultural land, as is evident from the decision of the *Primary Committee of the constitution of Land Estate Registry of the Community of Pigi, Konitsa* (10-9-1966). Now, while in the drawing up of the borders of the individual segments of the communal forest area it is declared that they border "privately-owned smallholdings", in the report we find that *within* the bounds of this area there are "privately-owned smallholdings". These segments, based on the diagram attached to the document are nos. 1, of around 490,000 m^2 at Mantziou-Kleftovrysi, 4 of around 870,000 m^2 at Palioronga and 5 of 260,000 m^2 at Trapezitsa. The borders, therefore, are not clear (besides, the Committee estimates the area at 3,840,000 m^2, while later (1975) in the management study of the Forestry Authority it is estimated at 2,000 m^2), but the presence of "privately-owned" smallholdings is evident within the borders of what is characterised as communal forest area. We will return to this.

Beyond this forest, however - the "Communal" one - there is also the publicly-owned one. Essentially, what is not communal is publicly-owned. And in this case, neither the borders nor the character of these areas are clear. This is why differences emerge in the local community and central administration regarding their use. I quote a characteristic extract from the Minutes of the Community Council concerning the use of one such area:

"1930. no. 2

On the waiving of a prohibitive order of the Forestry Administration on the pasture of Lioutsika, Plaka, Panagia etc. in Peklari

23rd December 1930

The Community Council of Peklari... lawfully met in Peklari on the 23rd of December 1930, heard its President, the opening topic of the waiving of a prohibitive order of the forestry administration on the pasture of the Community at Plaka-Panagia and, submitting the relevant prohibitive order no. 2 states that the Forestry Administration of Konitsa, unbidden and quite unjustifiably published and circulated its prohibitive order no. 2, in which it prohibits grazing and woodcutting for a decade in the pastureland of Lioutsika-Plaka-Panagia, for apparently protective reasons, and since this prohibition is purposeless and detrimental to the Community in limiting the grazing of its animals, he suggests the Council to raise an objection to it,

And being deliberated on

Since the Council finds the suggestion lawful and beneficial,

Since the above prohibition is considered completely purposeless and unjustified, as there is no main road in this place, but only a gully of the Topolitsa stream, out of which the animals can pass only in the summer for one or two months - for as long as the stream has no water. On the contrary the main road has passed above the gully since time immemorial, nor is there any other reason since there is no danger from grazing or woodcutting, since from time immemorial our animals have grazed there without doing any harm. Since it was wrongly and falsely reported in the prohibitive order that there are lime trees and other useful trees in the prohibited area. On the contrary, only useless bushes cover this area and in the main, moreover, it is made up of bare rocky and stony areas.

Since, with grazing prohibited in this place, the sheep and goats of our Community are completely cut off in the winter period since there is no other grazeable area for the domestic animals of our Community in the vicinity.

Since the above prohibitive order was published on bad and mistaken premises and information and not for reasons of real protection,

Decides

It unanimously appeals against the prohibitive order no. 2 of 30th of January 1930 by the Forestry Authority of Konitsa before the Ven. Gen. Administration of Epirus for the above reasons and

It asks the Ven. Gen. Administration to kindly take into consideration the above reasons and the needs of the Community and duly order the waiving and termination of the appealed prohibitive order, since it is catastrophic to the rearing of our domestic animals...". [39]

The publicly-owned forest, however, does not have clear boundaries in relation to the cultivated, "privately-owned" agricultural allotments. And in this regard the principle of dynamic permeation holds, depending on the conditions. When there is need for more cultivable land, agriculture comes into the forest. The practice of *trafokopima,* i.e. the expansion of fields by excavating the outer edges and extracting shrubs, stones etc., was practised until the 1970s (the stones were used for building terraces in the same fields, and the

---

[39] Community of Peklari. *Βιβλίον Αποφάσεων από 1ης Ιανουαρίου 1927 έως 31 Δεκεμβρίου 1933* (*Book of Decisions from 1st January 1927 - 31st December 1933*), pp. 74-76.

roots and branches as fuel).[40] When agriculture began to be abandoned, the forest extended onto the previously cultivated areas. Thus, these areas were not merely turned into forests but into publicly-owned forests under the law. Whatever ownership, which in any case was not safeguarded with official title deeds, was *de facto* cancelled. This was made easy by the abandonment and lack of interest from the inhabitants and in particular those inheriting these "properties".

The fields

The largest family would have six, seven, at most ten stremmata of fields. And it had them scattered over many places. Five hundred metres here, a thousand there, they weren't in one place. Back then, under the Turks, there were beys *here and they shared them out. The* bey *would come here and say: "You'll get five hundred metres here, you'll get another five hundred metres there..." There was no plain for you to get large fields... And so each family supported itself with the five or six stremmata that it had...* [41].

The trees were in one place and the irrigated fields were elsewhere. The fields were down below, at Mylos, there were three stremmata that I was given [as a dowry]. *Then there were some gardens up here, over near the house... the un-watered fields also had trees all around - a* kladaria. *For example, they would call the field at Machaira based on how many trees it had... if it had five trees, you had a* fortoma [lit. "load"]. *You would say,*

---

[40] Relevant information provided by the villagers Panagiotis Choupias, former president of the community, 76 years old, and Ioannis Spanos, retired teacher, 69 years old (interview 21-1-2-15).

[41] Antonis Tefos, retired craftsman, 82 years old (interview 23-3-2014).

you're getting two or three fortomata. *If you had a lot of trees, you would call it a kladaria, that is to say you would be putting three hundred handfuls on the* kladaria - *there were many trees. And in one place where there were many trees, there was no field, down here in Klisoura, there were three* kladaries. *There was no field there. It was all trees. At Mylos there was water. I was given a garden, down in Mentania... We also had a field on the road to Agia Paraskevi. That had water… My mother did not take that water out of the field. She would put all the manure from the animals there, leaves, straw. There was always water there. What beans, what courgettes, what grapes that field produced! Walnut trees all around, what walnut trees! We had whatever we needed. By the bucket-load. Potatoes, onions... now all that will go to the state. Now all that has become coppices. Now it is just for wood. But who will go there? They don't even allow it. Now they want papers from you. What papers?! No one has papers. It was all done by word of mouth... if the fields weren't farmed then others would take them and give whatever... they might have paid rent... Then there were fields and* kladaries *everywhere. Don't look now...* [42]

The above extracts of narratives by the villages show eloquently what we call the multi-fragmentation of cultivated land, which is combined with mixed farming and the corresponding agricultural practices (letting land lie fallow etc.). If we wanted to get a picture of the agricultural landscape of Peklari, as it was maintained up to the 1970s, we would have to dwell on the one hand on this fragmentation of agricultural plots and on the other hand on the morphology itself of the earth, which due to its sloping nature prescribes the construction of terraces, so that level surfaces can be created that are suitable for cultivation. We are speaking, therefore,

[42] Lefkothea Tefou, retired farmer, 74 years old (interview 11-1-2015).

of an agricultural landscape with fragmented, constructed and in certain ways enclosed fields, which characterises the zone around the village up to a certain altitude, which can reach a thousand metres or even higher in level mountain surfaces, such as for example at Mantziou, Palioronga and Trapezitsa. This area of fields in very mountainous points, far away from the village, demonstrates the great difficulty faced by the inhabitants regarding available cultivable land, a difficulty that compelled them to expand to the surrounding mountains in search of bare, level areas. The same difficulty, besides, led them to the practice of *xerongiasma* (clearing), which even the young inhabitants remember. The place name "Palioronga" (lit. "Old *Rongi*") is typical.

The mainly cultivated area is located around the village and is made up of the un-watered and irrigated fields. The un-watered ones are more mountainous, while the irrigated ones are located along the streams on both sides. Within the village and on its outskirts are the gardens, where garden produce is cultivated. Nowadays these are the only cultivated areas that have remained - to a very small extent, of course. Below the village, on both sides of the stream (Topolitsa) up to Boussi, on the borders of Konitsa, most of the irrigated cultivable areas are found, of which very few are cultivated today, mainly in the gardens next to the houses (the stream splits the village in two) and at Boussi, where we find a few crops for animal rearing.

In the fields -within them or at their edges- there are usually also fruit trees. Of these, apples and walnuts were also sold at market up to the 1970s. Moreover, in the fields there are often oak trees from which they obtain the branches to feed the animals in winter.

There are also, of course, agricultural plots in which oak trees dominate for this purpose -the *kladera*, a topic which we will deal with below.

This zone of fields, the zone of agricultural cultivation, also penetrates into the village in the form of gardens, and extends up to a point above the village where the forest begins. The boundary, as we have said, is unclear and fluid depending on the dynamic that develops at different times in the complementary forest-field relationship. Despite this, it is mentally bordered by three sacred points in the area, which are the chapels of Agios Athanasios, Agia Paraskevi and Agios Nikolaos. *There are three chapels around the village. Agios Athanasios, Agia Paraskevi in the upper quarter and Agios Nikolaos here in the cemetery. These three make a cross - a trivet, as they used to say. Probably to guard the village. That's how I judge it anyway...they are* dochia. *At the three* dochia *are three chapels. The* dochia *are passes, waiting points, how can I put it... The bandits took hold here. These parts are keys. A key here, a key there. They're dangerous parts. That's what our grandfathers would say. Keys...* [43].

The well-known encircling of the village, therefore, also includes the fields, which appear as an extension of the inhabited area, as a section of the domesticated and therefore consecrated space. On the borders of this zone the *kladera* are also located, placed within the fields, normally at the edges for obvious reasons. These trees, therefore, the oaks, are the "domesticated" trees compared with the "wild" trees of the forest, the pines and firs.

---

[43] Antonis Tefos (interview 23-3-2014).

The next productive circle in the area is identified with the boundaries of the communal land and consequently also includes the forests. Here the presence of chapels also has to do with the establishment-consolidation of borders (Ai Thanasis and Ai Lias on the border with Konitsa, Ai Minas on the border with Nikanoras etc), which were occasionally disputed and became the object of clashes and even legal battles between the communities, as for example in the case of the border with Konitsa at Ai Thanasis, where there were cultivated areas (Megachorafo).

Regarding produce, the basic crops, apart from garden produce and fruit trees, up until the 1970s were clover, maize, wheat, barley, oats, lentils. Earlier, there were also vines, mainly at Prosilio, whence the surviving name Ambelia Karagiannaion, which were abandoned after the War. Clover, maize, barley and oats were the animal feed, complemented by branches and grass. Beans, apples and walnuts as well as some animal feed were the main products sold at market. This involvement in the market economy, even in the most recent era of the 1970s, although it meant a monetising of the local economy, did not necessarily mean its commercialisation. According to our informants, they would sell some products so that they could buy the necessary oil and salt. This was not in a commercial context but a relative self-sufficiency. It is characteristic that all our interlocutors stressed the fact that they produced almost everything apart from oil and salt, which they bought.

The pastureland and the animals

It could be said that in some way the whole extent of the community is pastureland, in the sense that the different kinds of animals that are bred can graze anywhere - under specific circumstances and certain conditions. This does not mean that the use of the place for livestock is uncontrolled. On the contrary, it is under the strict control of the community both in relation to cultivated land and to the forests and *kladera*. I quote an extract from the Minutes of the Community Council (1927), in which it appears that the community regulates the manner of using the pastureland by establishing rules,

"No. 10: On the regulation and use of the communal Pastureland of Peklari, 8th May 1927.

The Community Council... decides

1) to cancel its act no. 7 regarding the regulation of pasture and the right of grazing

2) to organise the pasture of the Community of Peklari in this way:

a) Certifies as pastures of the Community the following: Machaira, Prosilia, Fteri, Pournia, Skrika with their various local names. All of the above pastureland will serve as pasture for all the animals of the Community of Peklari without exception over all the seasons of the year.

b) the Machaira pastureland is assigned particularly as a cattle meadow and only the Communit''s plough animals will graze there, as well as the sheep and goats of the inhabitants only from 20th May until 31st August each year. No other animal of the inhabitants or outsiders will be allowed to graze there.

c) in all the above pastureland, it is absolutely forbidden for animals belonging to outsiders to graze, and only 5 sheep or goats are permitted for each shepherd hired by the animal breeders for the grazing of their flocks.

3) To determine and enforce the grazing fees of all the animals of the inhabitants of the community, per person 4 drachmas for each small animal and 7 drachmas for each fat animal, for each season and for all animals excepting only those suckling their young. For the aforementioned shepherds from elsewhere, this fee will be doubled,

4) This act will hold for three years..."[44]

Qualitatively, pastureland is defined from the mountain meadows to bare regions, the pine and fir forests, the cultivated areas after the harvest and the *kladera*. There is large fluctuation in altitude, as the mountain slopes around the village have a steep incline and in some cases are precipitous. Both the forests and the extended bushy areas are prime pastureland for goats, and the bare areas for sheep. The fields and the *kladera*, when they are not cultivated, and after the harvest, are suitable for all animals. In the past, when animal breeding was the basic productive activity of the community, the pine and fir forests were limited to the higher altitudes and the precipitous slopes, and the deciduous trees were in the lower zones and did not grow: they were not protected, since the goats (mainly) would eat their crowns. The same was true of the forests, where they also grew deciduous trees, when the pasturing of flocks was permitted.

The prohibition against grazing in certain seasons, or its regulation by custom or by decisions of the community council, occurred precisely because it was aware of the negative impact it

[44] See Community of Peklari, Βιβλίον αποφάσεων από 1 Ιανουαρίου 1927 έως 31 Δεκεμβρίου 1933 (Book of decisions from 1st January 1927 to 31st December 1933), pp. 20-21.

could have on forests, which had to be protected for various reasons. Conversely, when a forest was not in danger, the presence of flocks could have beneficial consequences according to the inhabitants, in the sense that they "cleared" the forest and kept the footpaths open, in opposition to the state of desolation which arises with the abandonment of animal breeding and is thought of negatively.

Proof that the community land was more suitable for goats comes from the fact that over time the proportion of goats to sheep was 70:30. There were also the "fat" or "large" animals (cows, horses, mules and donkeys). For their pasturing there were special regulations in certain periods and seasons, as we saw above. It is characteristic that in the community area there is a place called Gaidourochorafo (Donkey-field), since they tethered the donkeys there to graze. In another place, at Karoutes, from where today the community is in part supplied by water, the cows were watered. This means that they also grazed there. From the stories of the inhabitants and the visible signs in the place, a dynamic system of managing the area, with regard to animal breeding, had developed. This made best use of the available pastureland and the other useful elements for feeding animals (fields, *kladera* etc.), based on the number of animals, the composition of the flocks and the balance in more general terms of animal breeding and agriculture, as well as the management of the forests.

Let us now see how a villager describes the system of animal breeding in the post-war period and up until the 1970s:

Each family had between 10-15 goats and 400-500 were gathered in each machalas [quarter]. *Each* machalas *had a shepherd. There were three* machalades, *three flocks. There was also a fourth* machalas *but it had few houses and they made a flock with another. The lower and upper* machalades *had separate flocks. Some shepherds were from the village but for the most part from elsewhere. Some were Vlachs, some were villagers who did that work. The flocks did not have separate pasture. They would change place. One day they would go over to Prosilio, the next to Agios Athanasios... to the various areas of pasture. There were also trees in the pastureland. There was* dusko [a species of oak], *hornbeam, elder, there was all the...there was* kladi [lit. branch]. *For we mainly had goats. Just a few sheep. The flocks were mixed but were mainly goats. Most people had 3-4 sheep and 10 goats, let's say. They didn't have more because they had work... The shepherd would whistle, eight o'clock in the morning, he'd whistle. He'd come out onto the ridge and whistle, "Bring your goats down to Ai Nikola. Bring out your goats to Agios Athanasios. Bring out your goats to Stichio"...*

All this area was grazed. The border was on the ridge. The border with Elefthero. There's a shrine there. Opposite is Prosilio. There the pines used to be small, now they've got bigger. Back then the goats would eat the pines and they didn't grow. There wasn't that much pine. But in time they take over... That place over there that looks like a ravine, do you know how good it is for goats... it has a variety of trees. It's got ash, hornbeam, elder, imero *[Valonia oak],* dusko *[oak]. The* dusko *[oak] has a broad leaf. It's not particularly fruitful, let's say, the goat or the ewe don't make a lot of milk, but the* blaguni [Hungarian oak] *makes a lot of milk. The* blagouni *is better, it becomes short with broad leaves. We say both* blagouni *and* dusko *[oak] in the old language... In the past the village had around 3000 sheep and goats. There were also the* tselingades [big herd-owners] *apart from the domestic animals. The Kitsos family...in winter they had them down in*

Boussi and in the summer up here. There were 4-5 families that had tselingata *[big herds]. And they had plots of land too.*

...in the winter the animals would eat klari [branches]. *The women would cut the branches and we would make kladaries. They would also sow some clover in the village, they'd harvest it and put it inside the hut and hole up for the winter*[45].

There were, therefore, two kinds of animal breeding. The domestic and the transhumant. The domestic concerned the few sheep and goats (mainly goats) which all families maintained in the framework of the agricultural-animal breeding economy of self-sufficiency. These made up the communal flocks, one per quarter of the village, which were driven up to the mountain pastures in the summer period by hired shepherds of the community. The transhumant kind concerned certain families who had property in the region of Boussi near Konitsa, where they spent the winter, and in the summer went up to the mountain pastures of the village. This is the well-known small-distance mobility, given that the flock can move from the mountain to the winter quarters in the same day. This kind of transhumant pastoralism is still continued by two families, with small differences with the past.

This is how one of the animal breeders, an inhabitant of Boussi, describes their way of life:

Winter here, summer in the village. In the past we used to go up in Spring. Now we go in June. We would come down when the weather got worse. October, November. Here they graze in the area of Peklari. From Sfagia to Ai Lia. On this side of the stream is ours, our property. Our grandfathers

---

[45] Antonis Tefos (interview 23-3-2014).

had bought it, with gold sovereigns. They were abroad somewhere. We, the Kitsos family, are many. There are also fields. Now they've abandoned them all. Other relations have got some too. But they abandoned them all and left to go abroad. To America, Germany... Here we grew everything. Maize, clover, wheat and barley. Everything -more for the animals. In winter we would feed them more with maize and clover. We also made kladaries. *We cut* dusko *[oak]. Women and men, we'd cut the branches and bring them down here with the animals. Our own trees.* Dusko, blagouni. *It's the same thing. It has a bigger leaf than the* imero *[Valonia oak]. We didn't cut* tsero [Turkey oak] *for* kladaries. *We'd put them out in* kladaries *or in the storehouse. All the animals ate these branches. We didn't cut much green wood in the winter. But the good-hearted shepherds always had an axe and they'd cut branches to feed their goats. In the winter they ate grass,* bitounitsa, tzilinia [*phillyrea*] *(it's like holm oak but doesn't have prickles), strawberry tree* [*arbutus unedo*], leniko [Greek strawberry tree]... Leniko *is very good, sweet. Now they eat a lot of hornbeam. The strawberry tree is quite bitter. They eat the prickly oak too, as long as it's dry. The kids get their teeth through that, too. There's one that is dry and another that has prickles... here the land is best for goats. There are lots of branches. Oak, hornbeam, Judas trees, dogwoods... the goats eat these, they nibble them and they're low. If they're hungry they eat everything. The cedars too. When they're soft they chomp through them. They eat pine, too. If they're hungry, if they don't find grass they'll eat the Judas trees. They don't eat the planes much.*

In the summer in the past they used to let us graze after the harvest. Before the harvest we'd graze where there were no fields. Afterwards, we didn't pay for grazing in the fields, they let us… When the village had domestic flocks we didn't go to their pastureland. We'd go higher up. We'd go very high up on the mountain. Left of Sousnitsa. Afterwards, when there were no flocks, and now, we go anywhere. We have the sheepfold at Limnes, opposite Plaka.

We were five siblings, three boys and two girls. We had 150 sheep. Then we bred them. When we separated [the boys], we took 100 each. Back then we bred only goats, because this place is [best] for goats. Now my son Kostas has 450 goats and Ilias has 300 sheep. They have them separately. In the summer they make their folds next to each other. They graze in the same area. In the summer it's better up there. It has better water. It's hot here. Each has an Albanian working for them, but they go too. I also help. I milk. I also go to the pastureland from time to time. We milk them twice, morning and evening. Separately. The lambs come early, but some come late. The early ones he sold at Christmas. Kostas has just sold the kids. We used to have three or four animals, we'd carry the milk, branches... Now we have a donkey and a mare. We don't need them now. They're useless...
[46]

The kladera or longaria

The sheep would eat grass, whatever there was on the ground, and the goats whatever there was in the trees. Oak, pine. Those, basically. They weren't big trees because they would eat them, the goats would nibble them and they wouldn't grow, they remained bushes... Of course, there were large trees in some fields, which each owner would prune and they would grow, every three years they would cut them, they'd gather thymonies *[haystacks], as we call them, and they would have them for animal feed in winter. These trees were inside people's land.* There weren't any outside.

---

[46] Nikos Kitsios, animal breeder, 75 years old (interview 18-4-2014).

They were in land with edges, walls, with... the fields were separated. These trees, which were dusko [oak], tseros [Turkey oak] and imero [Valonia oak], were at the edges of the fields,*where they grew various things, wheat, barley, vetch... Inside, in the main field, there were no trees -only at the edges, next to the border. If a tree was on the border they would cut it down, to avoid a dispute. Each of us, therefore, had what was in his border and every three years they would prune them. These trees were part of the property. They were inherited, given as dowries etc. In taking the field as an inheritance or dowry, you'd also get the trees. In the winter, when the animals remained inside, they were fed with these branches, clover or grass that we gathered from the fields that we farmed and, when the weather allowed the animals to go out, they would eat whatever greenery there was... These fields with the* kladaries *were property. That's what we called them. I had a field, if for twenty years no one claimed it then it was mine. This was the custom. There were no papers but there was respect, and still is. They knew that that field was Kostas', Nikos', Yannis'. End of story. No one went in to cut branches. If the owner didn't cut any, you could go in and cut them with his permission... He'd say to you, "you'll cut branches but you won't touch the main wood." He'd say, "there are five trees, I know, I remember, you'll go and cut the branches for your goats but you won't touch the trees". If the owner was away for years, you could go and take advantage, but you couldn't say "this is mine"...* [47]

To feed our goats for the winter, we had to make around thirteen kladaries. *For one* kladaria *you need between six and ten trees. We needed around sixty trees. And since we didn't have so many, we would go to Exochi. Our*

---

[47] Nikos Kefalas, former secretary of the community, now an employee of the Municipality of Konitsa, inhabitant of the village, 56 years old (interview 29-3-2014).

grandmother was from there, our mother's mother, and they had some trees and fields over there, and we would go two hours from here -what with children, animals and axes- and we'd cut 40-50 bundles, regular bundles, we couldn't carry them, and we'd load them up on the horses and bring them here and make a kladaria *afterwards, outside, right next to the pen. The pen had upstairs and downstairs, stone with a wooden floor. Upstairs was the shed and the animals below. Upstairs clover, straw... The* kladaria *outside. We'd put on some of the* kladaroxyla [wood for the kladaria], *as we'd call it, from plane or pine or whatever... We'd dig in the ground, as much as was needed inside, we'd add to the three-hundred handfuls, we'd say that now we had it ready (we'd leave it for a little for the branches to dry and not get ruined) and the next day, in the morning... This work went on after the village festival* [27th July], *after July we began to do it. Before the harvest, the threshing. That was when we did this work. Every animal load was 50-55 handfuls. For a* kladaria *you needed 300 handfuls. And to get through the winter one animal needed one* kladaria. *We'd put on the wood for the* kladaria *and then we'd lay down dry twigs from the previous* kladaries *so that the branches don't touch the earth (from the twigs of the previous year nothing went to waste, we would use them also for fire and the oven as kindling). Then we'd begin to put on the handfuls. With the stems facing outwards to get rid of the water, so that the branches do not get wet. We would slope the whole thing. From the ground we'd begin more broadly and then little by little make it narrower going upwards. At the top, for example, we'd reach around 5-6 handfuls all around. And on top we'd cover it with other different kinds of branches. The height depended on the number of handfuls. Some put on 500 handfuls... As it got bigger we'd climb up and stand on it. You'd climb up by standing on it. Someone else gave you material from below... as it went up it grew thinner, to let the water run off, and on top we'd cover it with various branches, whatever there was, Judas tree, plane... since our house was near the gully and there were planes, we would put plane branches on top. For each of us it depended on what we had. We did it to stop it getting wet. Then we'd cut* kloutsous, *as we called them -thick wood, fork-shaped, two or three which held the branches from the bottom. We'd put one here, one there, one there, we'd stand on them from above so that they didn't get blown over. And we'd sometimes put on a stone or two. From the weight it'd sit there, then squeeze together and the water ran off and the branches remained inside, green as can be. That was women's work. There were no men in the village. We didn't know any men in the village, they were all travelling. And the children also helped. Here the woman had the responsibility for the house, the children, everything. Milking, collecting the milk, kneading bread... there were no men... they were away. Travelling. They would leave at Easter and come back at Christmas. They were away during the agricultural work. Their job in the winter was going to the café and... having children. That was their work in the winter. In the summer, when the weather was good, the shepherd would take the animals out. But when the weather was bad -rain, snow etc.- they stayed in the cellar and ate dry feed. Each had his own. In the winter, when the animals go out -and still today - they eat green branches. We cut them too. Cedar, pine... They used to go down to Boussi and cut strawberry trees too... We'd also cut the mistletoe from the pine. That was for the kids. Everyone gathered fodder for the kids. We'd go to get something like that, for the kids to be born and for us to get some money to buy oil and salt. Back then we only bought oil and salt. We had the rest. We'd climb up the pines and gather the mistletoe. The women did it all. We'd climb. We'd leave branches there,* anevato, *we'd call them. For us to climb up. If they couldn't, they'd get their children and stand on their shoulders... and climb up. We rarely made* kladaries *out in the trees. We'd bring them here to the village, or to the threshing floors, to the pens, and we'd make them. In the winter it was a bother to go there to bring them back. If we did make them out there, we had special trees and they'd leave the wood for the* kladaries *and the branches at the bottom specially and you'd make the* kladaria *on it. At the end you would put the* kloutsous *on top and that was it. They'd make the trees like that from when they were small. They'd say "this one here is straight, let's prune it a little to make it into a* kladaria*", and every year it got bigger and became a* kladaria. *We'd prune every three years. Otherwise the branches didn't become good, the goats didn't eat them. We called it* malliarokladi [lit. hairy branch]. *It didn't manage to become a branch, to become shiny, for the animals to eat it. They wouldn't eat it. Three or four years [were needed]... And it didn't become big enough for you to bind it. The seedling that came out was small, you couldn't make it a handful to load it onto an animal or to hang it, nor could you make it into a* kladaria *nor could you dry it for them to eat it. They would grow the tree and as it grew they would cut a little further and further out. Then there was the head of the Forestry Authority. He would tell us to leave the tuft at the top. It was law for the crown to remain. We looked after the tree differently. But then we always had that man breathing down our necks. We used to cut all the crowns, but we wouldn't cut them completely. You would cut it properly on the tree. And the tree would grow afterwards. We ensured that it could spread out. So it got worse later, because the crown grew a lot and you had to cut it afterwards. We didn't ruin the trees, we wanted them too, to live... There was a large tree with many branches, he said "all this has to go apart from one branch". This branch then after three years became so thick. Having been a little thing, after three years it became like that. How could you get up there to cut it down? Wouldn't you need to cut it? It was worse... What difficulties we had then... to avoid being caught, them doing something to us... the villagers from there were on our back, too, because we'd go to other villages too* *and every village had its borders. We'd go, for example, to Trapeza. In Trapeza, just as we have the pine forest, there it's all oak. We'd go and cut them. If they caught us, sometimes they'd take our axes, sometimes they'd take us to the Forestry Authority... we'd do it on the sly... We'd go to Exochi more, where our grandmother was, but it was near there and we'd say, "why not let's cut one or two". And if they got wind of us... we'd cut with one axe. Our tools were axe and rope. We'd cut them, we'd gather them, we'd put them on our backs to carry them to a level area where we'd load them onto the animals. We wouldn't put anything on the load, the animal would hold up. We would usually put on sixty handfuls. Thirty on one side and thirty on the other. We'd put them in six piles of five handfuls each. We'd put the first on one side, the animal held up, right away we'd go to the other side, we'd put the same there and we'd keep going... If need be sometimes we'd also put a piece of wood for support, but usually the animal held up, we'd tighten the* brostneles *[ropes] on their feet and... We'd go to the land that wasn't farmed,* longaria *we'd call them, and we'd go more because they were low down and we could reach them, cut ever so quietly with our axe, make our handfuls and leave... Here you had to climb the trees, to be all day in them. My mother, since we didn't have means, did her day's work. She cut branches, she ploughed the fields... all that ploughing, sowing... you can't imagine. And when we were young and wanted to cut branches in the trees, our mother didn't let us climb. She was afraid that we'd fall. She'd say, "sit down, let me go up to cut, I'll do it quicker". She could do everything very quickly. Usually mother would cut, I'd bind and Nikos would carry.*

The oaks, the "trees" as we call them, are of many kinds. The tseros [Turkey oak] *is the one that has a narrow leaf. That tree that's in front of the church is called* tseros. *We didn't cut that one in the summer, we'd cut it in November, because the leaves were late to fall. They were late, and we didn't use it much, we didn't really gather it. It's not good for* kladaries. *It's better for eating there and then, green. We only made* kladaries *from* imero *[Valonia oak] and* blagouni *[Hungarian oak] which is the one with a broader leaf than the* imero. *We liked that because it's broad, the goats eat it. Those who had trees here and couldn't let them be ruined would use* imero, *but we used more* blagouni *from over there. We'd cut the* imero *more when the goats were giving birth, for the kids to eat. The leaf is smaller, more narrow and the kids eat it more easily. There is no* blagouni *here, it's rare to find a tree. Here there is* imero. *The* imero *becomes a fatter tree. The* blagounas *grows taller and... rots more quickly. The* imero *is a tougher tree, more sturdy that is. It is also better as firewood. Especially those that are old and have heart... the* tseros *spits, if you put it in the fire, it spits and jumps, It's no good, it might throw out coal and you'll be set alight. There aren't many* tseros *here. there are some, but they're old. They've left them all, they don't cut them. Here we have the* imero. *But now these are left as well, no one cuts them... no one makes* kladaries *now. Now whatever we bring we put in the sheds. We have fewer animals, too... I put them in the storehouse now...* [48].

The *kladera* were not simply an important factor in the local economy. They represented the link between agriculture and animal breeding, decisively contributing to the existence of the latter in a place where the climatic conditions, for several months of the winter period, do not permit the external grazing of animals and enforce the storing of food for the period when the animals are stabled. Their very spatial arrangement demonstrates this decisive role that

---

[48] Galateia Vourdouka, inhabitant of the village, 62 years old (interview 29-3-2014).

they had in connecting agriculture with animal breeding. The trees, normally oaks, are located on the edges of the fields and represent an inseparable part of them -from the point of view of "ownership", too. We don't find them on the boundaries of the fields, as generally happens with the division of property in agricultural space, but inside the fields, on the edges, and it is mentioned moreover that if a tree grew on the border, they would cut it down, to prevent disputes between the owners of the fields. Both this particular arrangement and the shape that these trees take, due to pruning and the attention paid to them more generally, constitute an important element of the shaping of the landscape in question.

Given that the natural environment of the community and particularly the flora is more suitable for goats than for sheep (that is why the proportion was 7:3) and given also that the goats are fed more with branches than grass, the need for the existence of *kladera* to feed the goats in the winter, when they cannot graze outside, is self-evident. More dried branches than grass were needed, therefore, and the amount depended on the number of animals that each family possessed. If we estimate that one goat needed one *kladaria* to get through the winter, and that for one *kladaria,* at least six trees have to be pruned, this means that if one family has 10 goats, at least sixty trees are required. If we consider also that the trees are only pruned every three or four years, the number of required trees multiplies. This creates the need for seeking branches outside one's property and the community area, as well as the use of evergreens (pines, cedars etc.), which are pruned in the winter and given green to the animals, i.e. on the same day as they are collected.

In this way a fluid and dynamic system of using the trees that have suitable branches for feeding animals is created, in which one looks for solutions of regulating the balance between the needs of the family, the number of animals needed and the available fields and *kladera*. Given that from one point in time onwards -during the post-war period- many fields, and therefore *kladera*, were abandoned due to emigration, this system became more relaxed, as the villagers who remained could exploit the abandoned *kladera*, normally with the permission of the "owners". Over time, and due to the afforestation of the abandoned fields, the ownership itself comes into doubt, with the result that it is easy for anyone to use them. We will return to the question of ownership below, in a separate chapter. The same situation is also formed in connection with the grass that they cut, dry and store for the winter, and which can be used in case of lack of branches and as fodder for the goats (although usually it is assigned to the sheep and large animals). Hay, in any case, provides an alternative solution to the problem of the winter feeding of animals and this makes the whole system even more flexible with regard to family survival strategies. Dry branches, however, undoubtedly provide the safest solution, because they are not at the mercy of climatic conditions, as grass is (drought, frost etc.) and, moreover, they are more resistant to time, since when stored in a suitable way in *kladaries* they can remain in optimal condition for some years.

The trees that make up the *kladera*, normally oaks, represent objects of "care" and protection, since they play a decisive role in the survival of the domestic group and the community more generally. It would never be a possibility to cut down this kind of productive tree. They are cut down only when they get old and rot, when they are used as fuel. The remains of the branches are also used as fuel (*tsakna*) after the use by animals. An understanding of the crucial usefulness of these trees has led historically to many kinds of protection, such as through religion (*vakoufika* - monastery property, *aforismena* - excommunicated) or collective decision on the prohibition of grazing, woodcutting etc. for some years of specific areas with such trees as can be developed and used later as *kladera*.[49] In the case of church *kladera*, the church committees can put the *kladera* up for auction, in order to put the proceedings towards relevant projects or charitable goals in general. Something of this kind was happened in Peklari until recent years.

Moreover, the various kinds of oak, which bear different names *(blagouni, imero, tseros* etc.), with their different characteristics give the capacity for a variety of uses. These facilitate animal breeding, depending on the season and the weather conditions. The narratives quoted above are characteristic. Let us reiterate, as an example, the case of the *tseros*, which is not used for *kladaries*, since its leaves are small and narrow and late to fall. They are used, therefore, in November, before they fall -green, that is- on the same day as they are pruned. In this way they are not compelled to use the

[49] For similar cases, see P. Halstead "Ask the fellows who lop the hay: Leaf-fodder in the mountains of Northern Greece", *Rural History*, 9, 2, 1998, pp. 211-234 and K. Stara, *Μελέτη και καταγραφή ιερών δασών και δασυλλίων στον εθνικό δρυμό Βίκου-Αώου* (*Study and record of sacred forests and groves in the Vikos-Aoos National Park*), PhD thesis, University of Ioannina, 2009.

branches stored in the *kladaries*, which are needed for the following months when deepest winter sets in.

Generally speaking, the *kladera* sum up the basic characteristics of the local economy from many points of view. Beyond the fact that they express the combination of agriculture and animal breeding, they are also linked to the energy needs of the community, since from them the necessary fuel is obtained (from the old trees, the remainder of the branches, even the dry leaves). Moreover, they can obtain wood for construction from trees that are cared for in the appropriate way. It is for all of these reasons that they constitute an important resource for the community, and an object of high protection. Moreover, in several cases they are protected through religious practices (*vakoufika*). The periodic nature of branch cutting and the crop rotation from year to year, as well as the practice of leaving fields fallow, suggest a system of "sustainability". This has been established over the years on the basis of the awareness of the limits of the local ecosystem and the corresponding natural resources, which must not run out, to ensure the prospect of survival in the family and community through the generations.

The question of ownership

From one's first visit to the village and first discussions with the villagers, the uncertainty regarding ownership can be perceived. The lack of interest from the villagers about their property apart from that which is within the village (i.e. the houses and gardens) is also telling. Then there is the fact that almost all of the formerly cultivated areas and *kladera* located in the broader community area are tending towards afforestation, and thus automatically, by law, go into the hands of the state irrespective of whether or not there are title deeds.

To understand this situation, one must look at the historical background of ownership relations, the broader context of relationships of production in its historical perspective, and the political economy in relation to ecology, i.e. the system and strategies of appropriation of natural resources in specific and historically defined contexts.

At first sight, the small or no interest shown by the villagers to their property, even those who continue to live in the village, appears odd to an outside observer, in a time of unchecked commercialisation of all elements of production and of course of the land. The shift from individual to public "ownership" through the expansion of forest, and the decree that former "properties" by law become public forests seem not to concern the "owners" much. That is why they do not take any relevant action (e.g. fencing the area, legal claims, legal safeguarding etc.). This is also true for the few cases of people who claim to have title deeds (the vast majority do not). At my asking whether they declare their property in their tax return, most said that it is not worth the effort, others mentioned that all those who had declared them now take them out, due to the new tax on real estate, and some gave ambiguous answers related to the uncertainty of the ownership situation. The interpretation of this fact, in my opinion, should not be limited to the fact that the village has been abandoned (and no one is occupied with agriculture and animal breeding) or with the absence of the prospect of touristic development, which could lead to a commercialisation of the land and thus to the abandoned "properties" acquiring added value, as happened for example in the Zagori. We should go to a deeper level, which concerns the collective mentalities and habits, interwoven with the self-sufficient society, as this functioned in the long period of Ottoman rule and continued to function until the 1960s-70s, with changes that did not influence the fundamentally self-subsisting character of productive relationships despite the monetising of the economy.

In order to understand this whole framework of collective mentalities, which characterised the community even after its integration into the Greek state and the relevant structures and mechanisms of the capitalist system, essentially until the era of the great exodus and the consequent abandonment of the village in the post-war period (1970-80), we must have recourse to the political economy of the Ottoman period and particularly to the system of land ownership and the broader framework of productive relationships.

In the Ottoman empire the land was, generally speaking, divided into five categories: State (*miriye*), dedicated to the church (*vaqf*), private (*mulk*), common (*metruke*) and dead or desolate (*mevat*). The state lands were divided into public and semi-public. In the semi-public, the state had the bare ownership and the usufruct belonged to individuals. Private property could only be buildings, gardens, orchards and later, vineyards and other agricultural land. This arose from the "obligation" of the Ottomans to recognise the prevailing land-owning models in the areas which they conquered, or from distributing land in the form of a gift to their supporters. This kind of ownership, at least in the early phase of the empire, concerned use and not ownership, which remained with the state. A number of the dedicated properties (*vakoufia*) were formerly private properties which were dedicated to churches and other foundations for charitable purposes.

Regarding the villages themselves, to the extent that their inhabitants had "owned" land (*mulkia*), they were called *kefalochoria* ("head villages"). Apart from the *mulkia*, there were also the semi-public estates, in which the inhabitants only had usufruct (*tesarouf*) based on a title that was called a *tapi*. These properties were under the control of a feudal lord (*spachi*) and the usufruct was transferred only by inheritance. Regarding the common land, i.e. the forests, pastureland, roads, springs etc., this belonged to the state and the communities had use of them. On the other hand, the villages in which the usufruct of the inhabitants in the semi-public as well as private properties went into the hands of a person (*aga, tsiflikas*), who used them as his sharecroppers or wage-earners were called *tsiflikochoria*. [50]

---

[50] On the Ottoman land-owning system, see H. Inalcik - D. Quataert, *Οικονομική και κοινωνική ιστορία της Οθωμανικής Αυτοκρατορίας (Economic and social history of the Ottoman Empire)*, vols. 1 and 2, Athens, 2008, V. Mouraftsieva, *Αγροτικές σχέσεις στην Οθωμανική Αυτοκρατορία (15ος-16ος αι.) (Agricultural relationships in the Ottoman Empire (15th -16th C.))*, Poreia, Athens, 1990, P. Sugar, *Η Νοτιοανατολική Ευρώπη κάτω από Οθωμανική κυριαρχία (1354-1804) (Southeast Europe under Ottoman rule (1354-1804))* , vols. 1 and 2, Athens, 1994, D. Siatras, *Αγοραπωλησίες ακινήτων στην τουρκοκρατούμενη Ελλάδα (Buying and selling of property in Ottoman Greece)*, Gnosi, Athens, 1992. Specifically on Epirus: G. Ars, *Η Αλβανία και η Ήπειρος στα τέλη του ιη' και στις αρχές του ιθ' αιώνα (Albania and Epirus at the end of the 18th and beginning of the 19th century)*, Gutenberg, Athens, 1994, M. Kokolakis, *Το ύστερο Γιαννιώτικο πασαλίκι. Χώρος, διοίκηση, πληθυσμός (1820-1913) (The last pashalik of Yannina: Place, administration, population (1820-1913))*, KNE-EIE, Athens, 2003. On the region of Konitsa: Ch. Goutos, *Η επαρχία Κόνιτσας και η Μόλιστα επί τουρκοκρατίας (The Konitsa district and Molista under Ottoman rule)*, Athens 2003.

If we examine with some care the historical sources and the relevant historiography, we will see that even in the case of the category of "private" land (*mulkia*), it is not ownership in the modern, western sense of the term, i.e. proprietorship of the land, but rather rights of use. This is the case at least for the first centuries of Ottoman rule and until the early 19th century. It is telling, for example, that out of the cultivable areas with fruit trees and vines that belonged to the category of *mulkia*, the "ownership" concerned the trees and the vines themselves and not the land. For precisely this reason, when there ceased to be plantations, then the land that was covered by them went over to the state.[51] This situation changed when the Ottoman system started to decline and, with regard to land ownership, the *tsiftlik* appeared, a transitional form of ownership between feudal and individual ownership of a modern type. This was a process that began from the 17th century and reached its peak in the 19th.[52]

Peklari, as I have already said, was a *tsiftlik* in the middle of the 19th century and appears to have been sold off at the end of the century (in 1874 it was not a *tsiftlik*).[53] The *tsiftlik* represents a tran-

---

[51] See indicatively P. Sugar, *op. cit.*, p. 209, D. Siatras, *op. cit.*, p. 70.

[52] On the *tsiftlik* see K. Karavidas, *Αγροτικά* (*Agricultural matters*), Papazisis, Athens, 1931, K. Vergopoulos, *Το αγροτικό ζήτημα στην Ελλάδα* (*The agricultural question in Greece*), Exantas, Athens, 1975, B. McGowan, *Economic life in Ottoman Europe (taxation, trade and the struggle for land, 1600-1800)*, C.U.P - Maison des Sciences de l' Homme, Cambridge-Paris, 1981, T. Stoianovich, "Land tenure and the related sectors of the Balkan economy, 1600-1800", *Journal of Economic History*, XIII (1953), pp. 398-411.

[53] See C Goutos, *op. cit.*, p. 40.

sitional socio-economic formation that is linked with the more general shift from feudalism to capitalism in the context of the Ottoman system. "The metamorphosis of the ancient military fiefdoms into private and hereditary estates was the basis on which later the *tsiftliks* appeared - new forms of land ownership in the conditions of incipient capitalist relations."[54] "From around the middle of the 17th century the feudal system began to decline, largely due to the weakening of central authority and the fact that the Empire's wars of conquest had stopped, in which the *spachides* (feudal lords) were taking part. In place of the state feudal lords, there gradually appeared the large private estates, the *tsiftliks*. Their owners obtained them either lawfully or, more often, illegally and using extra-economic procedures: forging title deeds, blackmailing the villagers to leave their land, and even their villages, in order for themselves to enjoy their benefit, etc.".[55] The *spachides*, therefore, gradually give way to the *tsifltik* owners and thus a large number of villages become *tsiftliks*. The last *tsiftlik* owner of Peklari, as has already been mentioned, was

---

[54] B. Cvetkova, "Η εξέλιξη του τουρκικού φεουδαλικού καθεστώτος από τα τέλη του ΙΣΤ' ως τα μέσα του ΙΗ' αιώνα" ("The development of the Turkish feudal system from the end of the 16th to the middle of the 18th century"), in S. Asdrachas (ed.), *Η οικονομική δομή των Βαλκανικών Χωρών (15ος-19ος) (The economic structure of the Balkans (15th-19th century))*, Melissa, Athens, 1979, pp. 89-112, p. 107.

[55] G.N. Nikolaou, "Η κοινωνική και οικονομική κατάσταση στην περιοχή της Κόνιτσας κατά την περίοδο της οθωμανικής κυριαρχίας" ("The social and economic situation in the region of Konitsa during Ottoman rule"), in V. Nitsiakos (ed.), *Κόνιτσα. Από την οθωμανική κυριαρχία στο Ελληνικό κράτος* (*Konitsa: From the Ottoman empire to the Greek state*), Municipality of Konitsa, Konitsa, 2014, pp. 15-57, pp. 44-45.

Resit Bey from Konitsa, from whom the village was bought out and became free.

Regardless of the individual forms of land ownership that prevailed over different periods, I believe that the most important thing is to understand the fact that the local society and economy for a long period of time functioned in a system of subsistence. Even in the period when we see a penetration into the market and some forms of monetisation of the economy, the local system of productive relationships does not change orientation, continues to be supported on the production of use values and the presence of money does not lead to the commercialisation of the means and relations of production. This is how Asdrachas describes the situation: "In sum we can accept, broadly speaking, that the economy, in its totality, is characterised by a strong natural sector which roughly holds for the majority of the population, a population that is predominantly peasant; the monetary sector is in effect mainly for the populations of the consumer centres which, in turn, are seen in the large urban centres and are spread over a typology that calls us to individual investigations and verifications. The extreme case is the human concentrations where the disproportion between the capacities of natural wealth-producing sources and the population potential leads to the emanation of monetary income through trade, shipping, overland transport and specialisation in crafts -which is often itinerant. The peasant economies themselves, the village economies, demonstrate a level of monetisation: it is orientated, however, more to the service of tax revenue than to the expansion and consolidation of commercial relationships in the process of agricultural production. Besides, the necessary commercialisation does not meet the demands of taxation and thus the possibility of creating net income is inhibited, resulting in debt and alienation of the villagers. This negative impact of the extra-financial monetising of the peasant economy has as a symptom the cutting off of the direct producer from the market, or more specifically, his limited participation in a preliminary stage of the market, in a system of prices that does not allow the realisation of net income in monetary terms."[56]

Any involvement in the market, therefore, and the circulation of money, do not automatically signify the commercialisation of the means and relations of production. When this process remains in the sphere of circulation and does not fundamentally influence the sphere of production, changes and transformations regarding the fundamental orientation of the local society and economy do not arise. The extra-economic compulsions, such as taxation, are not sufficient to shift the orientation of the production process in a commercial direction, and thus for the means and powers of production to be commercialised, i.e. to change the mode of production. A change like that would also mean the commercialisation of the land, i.e. the shift to pure forms of land ownership of the modern (capitalist) kind. This does not occur, not even in the case of the *tsiftlik*, which constitutes a transitional stage, a transitional form of land ownership between feudalism and capitalism. The *tsiftlik* is not

---

[56] S. Asdrachas, "Εισαγωγικό σημείωμα" ("Introductory note") in S. Asdrachas (ed.), *Η οικονομική δομή των Βαλκανικών Χωρών (15ος-19ος) (The economic structure of the Balkans (15th - 19th C.))*, Melissa, Athens, 1979, pp. 19-42, p.33. See also by the same author, *Οικονομία και νοοτροπίες (Economy and mentalities)*, Ermis, Athens, 1988..

in any way a modern institution, nor does it constitute a socio-economic formation of a capitalist kind.

The interest in our case, however, lies in the fact that, even after the abolition of *tsiftliks* and the transition to free, modern, private ownership, we cannot speak of transformations that establish a manifestly modern situation, where the land is commercialised and the relationships of production are determined by a new system orientated towards the production of exchange values, i.e. we cannot speak of regular integration into the capitalist mode of production, meaning the commercialisation of all dimensions of economic life and the full integration in a free market economy in the modern sense of the term. Rather, the long duration of the subsistence society and economy is extended into the phase of modernity, i.e. even after integration into the Greek state in 1913 it survived almost three decades after the Civil War (1946-49), essentially until the definitive exodus and abandonment of the village which came to an end in the 1970s-1980s.

Thus, both the broader framework and local mentalities give a blurred picture of the relationships of landed property. It is characterised by oral-customary functionality, fluidity of borders and boundaries and incompleteness of the commercial character of production. The domestic groups, after the buying out of the village from the *tsiftlik* owner, acquire land ownership, plots of land in various parts of the communal area, which can be inherited, sold etc., but the whole system is characterised by fluidity and dynamics also connected to family strategies with regard to the developmental cycle of the domestic groups. Since normally there are no title deeds and the system functions by codes of custom, it is natural for the fluidity which I am speaking of to be constituted in the extent of the borders themselves of a plot of land or in the creation of new fields arbitrarily, when the needs of the domestic group are increased, but it does not lead to clashes with other villagers (e.g. *xerongiasma* of forest sections). The fluidity is even constituted in the abandonment of "plots" when they are not necessary for the survival of the group[57]. In the case that some "plot" is abandoned for many years, based on customary right, anyone who has need of it can use it. This is the case both for fields and for the *kladera*. Nevertheless, it is also relative, as fallow fields or unused *kladera* are often used by third parties with or without permission from the "owners". This happened more often as the village was abandoned, particularly during the post-war period. All of this ultimately constitutes a system of continuous adjustment based on the needs of self-preservation and the survival strategies of the domestic group and the community, which also functions through a kind of social egalitarianism. When this system reaches its limits, then safety valves operate, such as the exodus of the male population to technical specialisation (itinerant craftsmen) or later to other professions (e.g. workmen, loggers). Of

---

[57] In the Minutes of the assemblies of the community councils there are recorded cases of "trespasses" on communal areas by villagers, which demonstrate these practices. I quote an indicative decision: *Subject: "On the ratification of the list of those owing rent due to the arbitrary occupation of communal land... that K.K., from our Community, occupied of his own accord and with no right whatsoever a Communal area (1) of around one stremma by the area of 'Lefto-Boussi' in the region of Pigi, and by the testament of the Community not only does not withdraw, but on the contrary has planted trees of his own accord..".* (*Minutes from 1958, no. 29*).

course, when the community reaches a deadlock, it is led to mass exodus and abandonment.

Strategies of survival, social egalitarianism and safety valves

Knowledge of the historical context in connection to the political economy, as I have already said, is a necessary condition for understanding survival strategies of the village as a whole as well as of the individual domestic groups that make it up, given its environmental context, i.e. the natural resources available for appropriation. Referring to political economy I am essentially speaking of the "mode of production" that characterises the economic, social and political system of a formation. In terms of "modes of production", much ink has been spilled in the social sciences and particularly in economic anthropology, where occasionally additions to the known modes of production have been suggested, such as "peasant mode of production" and "domestic mode of production". It is a great debate which is certainly not to be considered now. My opinion is that we need add neither the "peasant" nor the "domestic mode of production", since both are incorporated in broader modes. This broader framework defines their basic characteristics. To understand a rural society/community or a domestic group, therefore, what has most importance is the orientation of the relations of production and not the individual technical details. This orientation is basically defined by the existence or not of commercialisation, by the appearance or not of exchange values - processes which clearly are linked to the incorporation in and assimilation to the capitalist system.

In the long period of Ottoman rule, despite the changes and transformations, the feudal mode of production remains. Local societies are incorporated into it with the basic units being the domestic group and the community. In this context, irrespective of any differentiations, the productive process is characterised by its self-supporting orientation, which is not nullified (as we said in the previous chapter) by any extra-economic necessities (particularly of taxation) which lead to one or other degree of monetisation. In the context, therefore, of the co-articulation of the local economy with the broader feudal system, local structures and functionalities are significantly affected, without losing the orientation of self-preservation. They continue, therefore, to be based on the production and re-production of self-sufficiency.

The shift of the wider system from feudalism to capitalism is of interest. It is a process which constitutes perhaps the most important element of the disintegration of the Ottoman empire. This shift was a long and complex process. A symptom of it, as I have already seen, was the appearance of the *tsiftlik* in the rural areas. This lasted in the northern sections of the country until the first decades of the 20th century.

Although the penetration of commercial relationships had occurred much earlier in the area of this study, the formal incorporation into capitalism essentially began with the liberation of 1913. With regard to the mountainous areas, the interesting thing is that this shift does not lead to fundamental changes in relation to commercialisation. The mountain communities remain orientated towards self-sufficiency and the production of use values, although they partake in the broader system of the market and in a monetised economy. We can, moreover, maintain that incorporation into the Greek state leads them gradually to an absolute dependence and control by the central authority. This, combined with other factors (demographic pressure, tendencies towards urbanisation etc.) ultimately brings about their decline and abandonment. This process, however, was also a long one, and for the type of community which I am talking about, lasted over a century.

In a specific context of transition, but with the same natural resources, the community and domestic groups which make it up continue the fight for survival, re-adjusting the relevant strategies and re-defining both the internal and external relations. It has become clear that, irrespective of the changes in the broader context of incorporation, the attachment of the community to an economy of the production of use values, in a process of self-preservation, supports to a large extent a relationship of dynamic balance with its natural environment. This is linked to internal mechanisms of an interesting social egalitarianism. The absence of commercialisation of the production process is combined with the absence of private ownership through the whole period of Ottoman rule. This, along with the elasticity in use of natural resources, depending on need and governed by the need for them not to run out (based on the awareness that the survival and reproduction of the group depended on them), were elements that contributed to the formation and reproduction of a system of "social economy" for a long period. Under this system, natural resources are used based on the survival and renewal of the productive units in a dynamic equilibrium, which does not allow internal differentiation. Each unit, revolving around the production of use values, uses natural resources (fields, pastures, trees etc.) in a rather unclear state of ownership, where the extension of the use, the change or abandonment etc. are regulated based on the needs of production and reproduction of the group as well as of the society as a whole. The result is that a dynamic and fluid situation is formed, in the context of which there also operates the phenomenon of social egalitarianism. The differentiations within the community are small and normally related to the needs of each domestic group in relation to the phase of its developmental cycle.

The fluidity and uncertainty regarding the boundaries between the various forms of appropriation of the environment (farming, pasture, pollarding, woodcutting etc.), as well as regarding the status of ownership is combined with a very elastic system of more general use of the natural resources. When this system reaches its limits, the need for ways out arises, so that the available resources are not exhausted and the reproduction of the community put in danger. It is a system of spontaneous and experiential sustainability that is combined further with forms of social solidarity, a system that can exist not on the basis of an ecological conscience but of the awareness of the boundaries of natural resources and a collective mentality of solidarity, based mainly on the idiom of kinship but also on a community ethos. Both in oral history and in the minutes of assemblies of the community council, hints and memories are recorded of deeds of social solidarity by the community in favour of impoverished villagers. Social egalitarianism is confirmed as a rule with reference to exceptions of villagers who due to temperament did not meet the standard of the self-supporting family in the context of a homogenous community.

It will be obvious that I am not speaking of ideal situations but of phenomena of adaptation and strategies of survival and renewal in exceptionally difficult conditions, both natural and historical. There are, of course, cases and occasions of the overcoming of the boundaries, of conflicts and tensions, but mechanisms to face them exist. Often nature itself prescribes solutions, as for example in the case of land-clearing (*xerongiasm*a). As a technique, it is clear that it often has catastrophic consequences for the land (denuding of wooded slopes, erosion, degrading of the environment etc.). In these cases they abandon the fields in question so that they can reforest. Moreover, systems such as mixed farming and leaving land fallow avoid the exhaustion of cultivated land and ensure the production of necessary and alternative products in conditions of great poverty.

In this historical context of political economy and ecological adaptation, social egalitarianism is understandable, as the use of natural resources obeys an open and elastic system that is not defined by ownership of the land but from its use, and which is based on equal access of all to the communal resources according to each one's needs. The result is equal distribution in the appropriated resources on the principle of use and based on the survival and reproduction both of the domestic group and the community.

Nor does this reality become fundamentally different with the incorporation of the community into the Greek state and capitalist mode of production, since the co-articulation of the local economy with the wider system does not transform it. The local economy continues to be orientated towards the production of use values and self-sufficiency, which means that it is not commercialised, i.e. the capitalist way of thinking does not penetrate inside the local economy and society. It is a telling fact that even in the cases where exodus from the community leads to enrichment -which is rare- money is never pumped into the local economy in the form of investment. In the only case of a merchant in the early 20th century who grows rich in Romania - Karagiannis- the money that comes into the village takes the form of beneficence, with the construction of works of common benefit, such as the stone bridge at the south-west tip of the village. One of the women of the village who I spoke to told me characteristically that her grandfather had become rich in foreign lands during the mid-war period, and following the advice of a lawyer, he had put the money that he had saved in the bank. In the end he lost it during the Nazi Occupation[58]. Any monetary capital, therefore, that arose through emigration was never brought back into the community in the form of economic investment. This explains the survival until recent years, when the community was a living organism, i.e. until the 1970s, of a system that functioned on the borders of capitalism in terms of self-sufficiency, despite the fact that it partook in many ways of the market economy.

Technical specialisation and "kurbeti" (emigration)

In previous chapters, when referring to the mountain communities during the Ottoman period, I highlighted the possibility of exodus,

---

[58] Anna Spanou (Karagiannis lineage), retired farmer, inhabitant of the village, 78 years old (interview 7/12/2014).

revolving around technical specialisation[59] but later around emigration itself, when economic difficulties and demographic deadlock arise. Thus, local systems have safety valves and there is always the possibility of lowering pressure on the finite natural resources and ultimately of the survival both of local societies and of local ecosystems.

In Peklari, we find the turn to technical specialisation (stonemasons), an activity which complements the agricultural-animal breeding foundation of the local economy and is practised exclusively by men until the definitive disintegration of the community in the 1980s. Let us see how one woman summarises the whole system during the final phase of its existence: *Back then we didn't buy anything. We even had flour. Just salt and oil [we bought]. A family lived with these fields and the animals. It was difficult, though. And the man*

---

[59] The oldest inscription of the surname of a craftsmen from the region of Konitsa dates to the year 1740. This means that the turn to technical specialisation occurred somewhat earlier. See A. Petronotis - V. Papageorgiou, *Μαστόροι χτίστες από τα Μαστοροχώρια της Κόνιτσας* (*Master builders from the Mastorochoria of Konitsa*), vol. 1, Ioannina Prefecture - Epirus A.E., Ioannina, 2008, pp. 26-27. In Peklari the first written evidence that we know dates from 1887. See M. Tsoupi, *Ηπειρώτικα λιθόγλυπτα. Τέχνη και κοινωνία. Ανιχνεύοντας στο Ζαγόρι* (*Epirote stone carving: Craft and society. Looking for traces in the Zagori*), Efyra, Ioannina 2006, p. 36. From oral tradition it appears that the mass turn occurred in the middle of the 19th century. See also A. Petronotis - V. Papageorgiou, *Μαστόροι χτίστες από τα Μαστοροχώρια της Κόνιτσας* (*Master builders from the Mastorochoria of Konitsa*), vol. 2, forthcoming, pp. 890-899.

[would be] a worker, a craftsman... We also had a few who went woodcutting. Many combined the two. But they too came in the evening and left in the morning. That is why the women did everything.[60]

Before moving onto the description of the local system after the turn of the male population to technical specialisation, it will be useful to give an outline of the historical context through which arises the need for exodus. As in the other communities of the mountainous area of the Pindos, the recourse to technical specialisation is combined historically with economic and demographic difficulties, which arose after its formation into a single and compact demographic and social entity out of the settlements scattered in the wider area of the community, of extended domestic groups of a patriarchal character. This happened gradually during the first centuries of Ottoman rule and is owed mainly to the political, administrative and fiscal elements of the system. With the concentration of the population and its natural increase, as well as external compulsions (taxation etc.), the need for additional economic resources was created. The local populace sought these in complementary activities, which led to a kind of exodus of the male population, an exodus that for a long period of time demonstrates the characteristics of the seasonal journey, based on the exercise of a technical activity -a craft.

We are not in a position to know how much the change of the village into a *tsiftlik* bolstered or halted this process, but it appears that it was an additional exogenous factor that accentuated the local recession, as the conversion of the community into a *tsiftlik*

[60] Galateia Vourdouka (interview 29-3-2014).

meant more tax obligations and consequently a strengthening of the exploitative mechanisms by the owner of the *tsiftlik* in overworking the inhabitants of the village. A development of this kind obviously strengthened the tendencies of exodus towards a search for complementary resources, in order to cover the increased needs that arose from the mandatory *dosimata* (rent) to the owner of the *tsiftlik*. In any case, following the sale, and for a long period of the liberated life of the community (in the Greek state), essentially until its final disintegration during the 1980s, the craftsmen's travel represented the fundamental complementary source of income for the domestic groups. The foundation of the local economy remained agriculture-animal breeding, which on the basis of the gendered division of labour was practised by the women, while the men, apart from practising itinerant crafts, from one point onwards (in the latter years) also took to woodcutting, which developed on a cooperative basis in the village. They also adopted other activities on a seasonal and occasional basis, usually outside the community, in Konitsa, Ioannina or in other urban centres. Emigration of the male population on a permanent basis at the end of the 19th century and the beginning of the 20th is not seen on a large scale, in contrast to other villages of the area, where this kind of process influenced communities on a significant level. Something similar occurred during the post-war period, the 1960s-70s, when we have a wave of emigration to Germany and to Australia. This exodus, however, is parallel to internal emigration and is intensified in the context of a generalised departure that began with the Civil War (1946-49) and in a short amount of time led to the abandonment and disintegration of the productive and social network of the community.

The fact, therefore, that in Peklari we do not have a large wave of emigration at the end of the 19th and beginning of the 20th century, which could lead to an internal economic and social differentiation within the community, added to the fact that no category of *tsiftlik*-owners arose, as for example in Pyrsogianni and Vourbiani, rule out the appearance of social stratification within the community through internal or external mechanisms. Thus, based also on the safety valves of exodus towards search for complementary resources for the subsistence of the domestic group, particularly technical specialisation, the community reproduces itself for a long period of time with no difference regarding the orientation towards self-preservation, nor internal economic or social difference. On the contrary, it reproduces itself on the basis of the relative self-sufficiency and egalitarianism which I described above.

Regarding technical specialisation, the craft of the itinerant stonemason, it is worth mentioning something else, because in this framework too we find elements of "moral economy", since the "intrinsic morality" of kinship plays an important role in the formation and functioning of agglomerations (*bulukia*) of the craftsmen in the practice of the activity in question.

The *bulukia* are formed essentially of craftsmen from the same community, and their basic core is usually made up of individuals connected by bonds of kinship. The social context, therefore, in which the *bulukia* of the craftsmen are formed is the community, and here kinship relations play a decisive role. Each master builder, therefore, seeks co-workers from within his family and the wider group of kin (*soi*). Indeed, it has been suggested that this situation decisively contributed to the presence of the extended family or domestic group, as the needs of the *bulukia* delayed the breakdown of families based on their developmental cycle, thus favouring the formation and reproduction of extended households[61].

This fact, given also that the groups of craftsmen comprise principally contractual forms of labour organisation, demonstrates that a "pre-modern" social bond, that of kinship, continues to function in a transitional context such as that of the *bulukia*. Indeed, it determines its structure, as well as the content of its internal relationships to a large extent, which revolve around the moral dimension of kinship. We dealt with this topic in detail in a previous article[62]. Here we can merely refer in summary to the importance of this phenomenon with regard to the social or moral dimension of the economy. The interest, therefore, of the phenomenon of the contribution of kinship to the formation and functioning of the agglomerations of craftsmen lies in the fact that its moral content also determines to a large extent the internal relationships of the group of co-workers. In other words, the "intrinsic morality of kinship"[63] - well-

---

[61] See E. Alexakis, "Ο κύκλος ανάπτυξης της οικιακής ομάδας στην ορεινή κοινότητα της Καστάνιανης Κόνιτσας" ("The cycle of development of the domestic group in the mountain community of Kastaniani, Konitsa"), in V. Nitsiakos - C. Kasimis (eds.), *Ο ορεινός χώρος της Βαλκανικής. Συγκρότηση και μετασχηματισμοί* (*The mountain region of the Balkans: Formation and transformations*), Plethron - Municipality of Konitsa, Athens, 2000, pp. 119-147.

[62] See V. Nitsiakos, "Συγγένεια και σχέσεις παραγωγής στα μπουλούκια των μαστόρων της Ηπείρου" ("Kinship and productive relationships in the bulukia of the craftsmen of Epirus"), Ethnologia, 8 (2000), pp. 5-13.

[63] See M. Bloch, "The long term and the short term: The economic and political significance of the morality of kinship", J. Goody (ed.), *The character of kinship,* C.U.P., Cambridge, 1973, pp. 75-87.

known in social anthropology - is used in the context of the *bulukia* for constructing relationships of trust and preventing wrongdoing. Generally speaking, we can argue that the moral bond of kinship is conducive to the production and re-production of a framework of moral economy in a situation in which purely economic relationships, with the modern meaning of the term, could be formed, of an economy which is not integrated into nor influenced by social relationships.

The technical specialisation and the seasonal travel of the *bulukia* of craftsmen represented, historically, the basic safety valve for the reproduction of the domestic group and the community, and decisively influenced the character of the village, turning it into a *mastorochori* (craftsmen-village). The foundation, however, remains agriculture and animal breeding. This goes almost exclusively into the hands of the women, through the gendered division of labour, where the men go out into *kurbeti*, practising their craft on a seasonal basis. Regarding the local productive activity of agriculture and animal breeding, they play a secondary role. This development also marks the rhythms of the social life of the community based on the absence of men normally from Spring to Christmas (the two time periods are normally defined from the *Apokries* (Carnival) when the craftsmen leave, and Christmas when they return). When the journey is to a nearby place, this rhythm changes, as the craftsmen can visit the village more often (whenever they are without work or they are needed in the village). In the latter case, which occurred more often in recent years, thanks also to the changes in modes of transport, the men can participate more in agricultural-animal breeding activity. In any case, we should not forget the complementary nature of the technical activity, and of course the fact that by itself it is not sufficient to overturn the character of the local economy, which remains orientated towards self-preservation, despite the monetisation of economic exchanges in the external relationships of the inhabitants. The role of woodcutting must also be further stressed, which retained part of the male population in the village, with the founding of the Forestry Cooperative in 1945 and the systematic exploitation of the forest from 1952[64].

We must also say that this exodus of the male population, along with emigration, gradually shape a new framework of diaspora, whence arise possibilities and potential of changes. Although these influence the local community in many ways and contribute to its reproduction, as we will see in the next chapter, they do not lead in any way to its transformation. In other words, they do not avert its productive and social disintegration, which is the end product of the long process of incorporation into the national economy and society.

---

[64] See the Forestry Archive of Konitsa, *Διαχειριστική μελέτη κοινοτικού δάσους Πηγής* (*Management study of the communal forest of Pigi*), Konitsa, 1975, pp. 9-10, whence also the statistic that in 1975 the Forestry Association numbered 13 members, of which 10 were active.

EPILOGUE

THE END OF A *LONG DURÉE*

In 1958, when the well-known Greek-French ethnographic research on the villages of Konitsa occurred, the researchers found themselves faced with their impending extinction[65]. Thirty years later, in 1988, the researchers of another project, a continuation of the previous one, noticed that these villages not only had not disappeared, but continued to exist in spite of the times. They were dying, but reproducing themselves in a curious way "outside themselves", economically with the help of remittances of the expatriates, and demographically by the return of retired people to spend the rest of their lives in the village. This phenomenon was called "demographic paradox" and the communities themselves "societies from a distance, primarily ideological and symbolic"[66].

---

[65] See E. Mentras, "Κοινωνιολογική διερεύνηση τριών πεδινών και τριών ορεινών κοινοτήτων της περιοχής Κονίτσης" ("Sociological investigation of three lowland and three mountain communities in the region of Konitsa"), *Ipeirotiki Estia*, 8, 9, 1959-1960.

[66] See E. Mentras, "Πρόλογος" ("Prologue"), in S. Damianakos - E. Zakopoulou - C. Kasimis - V. Nitsiakos, *Εργασία, εξουσία και μνήμη σε τρία χωριά της Ηπείρου. Η τοπική δυναμική της επιβίωσης (Work, power and memory in three villages of Epirus: The local dynamics of survival)*, Plethron, Athens, 1997, pp. 11-12.

In another paper I have dealt with the symbolic reproduction of the community after its productive, social and demographic disintegration to the diaspora, with the example of Pyrsogianni. Here I refer to that phenomenon, which is also observable in Peklari, in order to note -another thirty years on - the endurance of a dying community that reproduces itself outside the place and is maintained essentially by pensions, remittances and the meagre income from the only productive activity, woodcutting, along with a few traces of a domestic animal breeding and the basic cultivation of some gardens to secure garden produce for the year by the few couples of the fundamentally elderly inhabitants of the village. The heart of the community now beats more outside the village, in Konitsa, Ioannina, Athens and elsewhere - in any case in the diaspora - and the rhythm of its life depends decisively on the "coming and going" of emigrants, which is seasonal and varies depending on distance. The fact that a number of villagers have settled in Konitsa, where they have set up their own neighbourhood - Peklaritika - contributes substantially to the maintenance of frequent contact of the villagers with their village and consequently to the existence of mobility throughout the year. The presence, moreover, of the Cultural Association which organises events at regular intervals, strengthens this mobility to a large extent.

Nevertheless, the village gives the impression of abandonment for the largest part of the year. This abandonment is reflected in the most eloquent way in the recovery of nature and particularly in the increasing afforestation of areas that were previously cultivated. It is the end of a long era, that of an agrarian-animal breeding community of self-preservation that supplemented its resources with technical specialisation of the male population, and exodus to *kurbeti*. The inhabitants of the village call this phenomenon of the "recovery" of nature at the expense of human productive activity and presence *erimia* (desolation). The characteristic phrase they use is *rimaxe o topos* (the place is devastated), when they speak of this, and they are obviously referring to human desolation. The afforestation of abandoned fields, the closing of footpaths by bushes, the intrusion of weeds into dry stone walls and threshing floors, the expansion of forest areas towards the settlements, the "drowning" of huts, warehouses, sheepfolds etc. by brambles, thorns, nettles and other plants that thrive where there is abandonment -phenomena that from the perspective of a specific ecological approach mean the recovery of a previously "strained" natural environment - are understood in a completely different way, as they are linked to the historical collapse of the local economy and society and the desolation of the place in general.

BIBLIOGRAPHY

Athanasakis, A., *Περιβάλλον και Οικολογία στην Εκπαίδευση* (*Environment and Ecology in Education*), Dardanos, Athens, 1996.

Alexakis, E., "Ο κύκλος ανάπτυξης της οικιακής ομάδας στην ορεινή κοινότητα της Καστάνιανης Κόνιτσας" ("The cycle of development of the domestic group in the mountain community of Kastaniani, Konitsa"), in Nitsiakos, V. - Kasimis, C. (eds.), *Ο ορεινός χώρος της Βαλκανικής. Συγκρότηση και μετασχηματισμοί* (*The mountain region of the Balkans: Formation and transformations*), Plethron - Municipality of Konitsa, Athens, 2000, pp. 119-147.

Aravantinos, P., *Χρονογραφία της Ηπείρου* (*Chronicle of Epirus*), vol. 2, Athens, 1856.

Ars, G., *Η Αλβανία και η Ήπειρος στα τέλη του ιη' και στις αρχές του ιθ' αιώνα* (*Albania and Epirus at the end of the 18th and beginning of the 19th century*), Gutenberg, Athens, 1994.

Asdrachas, S., *Οικονομία και νοοτροπίες* (*Economy and mentalities*), Ermis, Athens, 1988.

Asdrachas, S., "Εισαγωγικό σημείωμα" ("Introductory note") in S. Asdrachas (ed.), *Η οικονομική δομή των Βαλκανικών Χωρών (15ος-19ος)* (*The economic structure of the Balkans (15th - 19th C.)*), Melissa, Athens, 1979, pp. 19-42.

B. Cvetkova, "Η εξέλιξη του τουρκικού φεουδαλικού καθεστώτος από τα τέλη του ΙΣΤ' ως τα μέσα του ΙΗ' αιώνα" ("The development of the Turkish feudal system from the end of the

16th to the middle of the 18th century"), in S. Asdrachas (ed.), *Η οικονομική δομή των Βαλκανικών Χωρών (15ος-19ος) (The economic structure of the Balkans (15th-19th century))*, Melissa, Athens, 1979, pp. 89-112.

Dalkavoukis, V., *Η πένα και η γκλίτσα. Εθνοτική και εθνοτοπική ταυτότητα στο Ζαγόρι τον 20ο αιώνα* (*The pen and the shepherd's crook: Ethnic and ethno-topic identity in the Zagori in the 20th century*), Odysseas, Athens, 2005.

Forestry Authority of Konitsa, *Διαχειριστική μελέτη κοινοτικού δάσους Πηγής* (*Management study of the communal forest of Pigi*), Konitsa, 1975.

Dasoulas, T., *Αγροτικές κοινωνίες του ορεινού χώρου κατά την οθωμανική περίοδο. Ο γεωργικός κόσμος της χώρας Μετσόβου (18ος αι. 19ος αι.)* (*Farming societies of the mountain region during the Ottoman period: The agricultural world of the land of Metsovo (18th - 19th century)*, PhD thesis, Ioannina, 2009, pp. 229-247.

Dafis, S. *Δασική οικολογία* (*Forest ecology*), Giachoudis-Giapoulis publications, Thessaloniki, 1986.

Dekleris, M., "Ο Τριακονταετής πόλεμος των δασών: το μέτωπο της Δικαιοσύνης" ("The Thirty Years' war of the forests: The judicial front"), http://www.oikipa.gr/index.php/-mainmenu-63/118-asi (6/10/2014).

Efthymiou, A., "Η Πηγή (Πεκλάρι)" ("Pigi (Peklari)"), *Konitsa*, 9, 1963, pp. 8-9.

Fanitsios, V., *Το δασικό ζήτημα* (*The forest question*), Athens, 1959.

Goutos, C., *Η επαρχία Κόνιτσας και η Μόλιστα επί τουρκοκρατίας* (*The Konitsa district and Molista under Ottoman rule*), Athens, 2003.

Grispos, P., "Δασική λαογραφία" ("Forest folklore"), *Ipeirotiki Estia,* 16 (1967), 19 (1970).

Grispos, P., "Το κουρί στην 'Ηπειρο" ("The *kouri* in Epirus"), *Ipeirotiki Estia,* May 1952, pp. 199-203 and July 1952, pp. 296-299.

Grispos, P., *Δασική ιστορία της νεωτέρας Ελλάδος* (*A history of forests in modern Greece*), Ministry of National Economy, General Directorate of Forests, Athens 1973

Hatzimichali, A., *Σαρακατσάνοι* (*Sarakatsans*), vol.1-2, Athens, 1957.

Inalcik H. - Quataert, D. *Οικονομική και κοινωνική ιστορία της Οθωμανικής Αυτοκρατορίας* (*Economic and social history of the Ottoman Empire*), vols. 1 and 2, Athens, 2008.

Ispikoudis, I., Sioliou, M.K., "Το πολιτισμικό τοπίο της περιοχής Πορταϊκού- Περτουλίου της Νότιας Πίνδου" ("The cultural landscape of the Portaikos - Pertouli region of the Southern Pindus"), *Geotechnika Epistimonika Themata,* 2, 15, 1, 2004, pp. 37-45.

Ispikoudis, I., "Ιστορική και πολιτισμική θεώρηση των δασογεωργικών συστημάτων" ("A historical and cultural view of forest-agricultural systems"), *Proceedings* of *Helexpo Zootechnia,* Thessaloniki, 3-6 February 2005, pp. 28-40.

Kapetanios, A., "Η περιπέτεια του ορισμού του δάσους" ("The adventure of the definition of forest"), http://dasarxeio.com/2014/06/14/605/

Karavidas, K., *Αγροτικά* (*Agricultural matters*), Papazisis, Athens, 1931.

Karamanes, E., *Οργάνωση του χώρου, τεχνικές και τοπική κοινότητα στα Κοπατσαροχώρια των Γρεβενών* (*Spatial organisation, techniques and local community in the* Kopatsarochoria *of Grevena*), Academy of Athens: KEEL, Athens, 2012.

Katsougiannis, T., *Περί των Βλάχων των ελληνικών χωρών* (*On the Vlachs of Greek lands*), IMHA, Thessaloniki 1966.

Community of Peklari, *Βιβλίον Αποφάσεων από 1ης Ιανουαρίου 1927 έως 31 Δεκεμβρίου 1933* (*Book of Decisions from 1st January 1927 - 31st December 1933*).

Kokolakis, M., *Το ύστερο Γιαννιώτικο πασαλίκι. Χώρος, διοίκηση και πληθυσμός στην Τουρκοκρατούμενη Ήπειρο (1820-1913)* (*The last* pashalik *of Yannina: Place, administration, and population in Ottoman Epirus*), PhD thesis, Athens, 1993.

Kontogiorgis, G.D., *Κοινωνική δυναμική και πολιτική αυτοδιοίκηση. Οι ελληνικές κοινότητες της τουρκοκρατίας* (*Social dynamics and political self-rule: Greek Communities under Ottoman Rule*), Nea Synora, A. Livanis Athens, 1982.

K. Lazaridis, *Η ατομική ιδιοκτησία στο Ζαγόρι (ή μια πλευρά του δασικού μας ζητήματος)* (*Individual ownership in the Zagori (or one side of the forest question*), Ioannina, 1972.

Loukopoulos, D., *Ποιμενικά της Ρούμελης* (*Pastoral Roumeli*), I. Sideris, Athens, 1930.

Loukopoulos, D., *Αγροτικά της Ρούμελης* (*Agricultural Roumeli*), Athens, 1938.

Maurer, G., *Ο ελληνικός λαός* (*The Greek people*), Tolidis, Athens, 1976.

Maris, G. - Karatasiou, M., - Stara, K., "Το 'κουρί' στο Ζαγόρι της Ηπείρου και η σύνδεσή του με τα δασολιβαδικά οικοσυστήματα" ("The 'kouri' in the Zagori of Epirus and its link with the forest-rangeland ecosystems"), *Proceedings* of the 16th Forestry Conference. Greek Forestry Association, Thessaloniki, 2013, pp. 747-752.

Mentras, E., "Πρόλογος" ("Prologue"), in Damianakos, S. - Zakopoulou, E. - Kasimis, C. - Nitsiakos, V., *Εργασία, εξουσία και μνήμη σε τρία χωριά της Ηπείρου. Η τοπική δυναμική της επιβίωσης* (*Work, power and memory in three villages of Epirus: The local dynamics of survival*), Plethron, Athens, 1997, pp. 11-12.

Mentras, E., "Κοινωνιολογική διερεύνηση τριών πεδινών και τριών ορεινών κοινοτήτων της περιοχής Κονίτσης" ("Sociological investigation of three lowland and three mountain communities in the region of Konitsa"), *Ipeirotiki Estia,* 8, 9, 1959-1960.

Mouraftsieva, V., *Αγροτικές σχέσεις στην Οθωμανική Αυτοκρατορία (15ος-16ος αι.)* (*Agricultural relationships in the Ottoman Empire (15th -16th C.)*), Poreia, Athens, 1990.

Nikolaou, G.N., "Η κοινωνική και οικονομική κατάσταση στην περιοχή της Κόνιτσας κατά την περίοδο της οθωμανικής κυριαρχίας" ("The social and economic situation in the region of Konitsa during Ottoman rule") , in V. Nitsiakos (ed.),

Κόνιτσα. Από την οθωμανική κυριαρχία στο Ελληνικό κράτος (*Konitsa: From the Ottoman empire to the Greek state*), Municipality of Konitsa, Konitsa, 2014, pp. 15-57.

Nitsiakos, V., "Από την κοινωνιοδημογραφική αποσύνθεση στη συμβολική ανασυγκρότηση και τη διαχείριση της κοινωνικής μνήμης. Η περίπτωση της Πυρσόγιαννης" ("From socio-demographic disintegration to symbolic reconstruction and management of social memory: The case of Pyrsogianni"), in: *Οι ορεινές κοινότητες της Βόρειας Πίνδου. Στον απόηχο της μακράς διάρκειας* (*Mountain communities in the Northern Pindos: In the echoes of the long durée*), Plethron, Athens 1995, pp. 79-132.

Nitsiakos, V. - Arapoglou, M. - Karanatsis, K., *Νομός Ιωαννίνων. Σύγχρονη πολιτισμική γεωγραφία* (*Prefecture of Ioannina: Contemporary cultural geography*), Ioannina Prefecture Government, Ioannina 1998.

Nitsiakos, V., "Συγγένεια και σχέσεις παραγωγής στα μπουλούκια των μαστόρων της Ηπείρου" ("Kinship and productive relationships in the *bulukia* of the craftsmen of Epirus"), *Ethnologia*, 8 (2000), pp. 5-13.

Νιτσιάκος Β., *Χτίζοντας το Χώρο και το Χρόνο*, Οδυσσέας, Αθήνα, 2003.

Nitsiakos, V., *Οι ορεινές κοινότητες της Βόρειας Πίνδου. Στον απόηχο της μακράς διάρκειας* (*Mountain communities of the Northern Pindus: In the echoes of the long durée*) Plethron, Athens 1995.

Nitsiakos, V. (ed.), *Η Κόνιτσα και τα χωριά της. Πολιτισμού ανατομή* (*Konitsa and its villages: An Anatomy of Culture*), Prefecture of Ioannina - Epirus A.E., Ioannina, 2008.

Oikonomopoulos, A., *Η εξέλιξις της δασοπονίας εν τη νέα Ελλάδι. Από της απελευθερώσεως αυτής μέχρι του έτους 1940* (*The development of forestry in modern Greece. From Liberation until 1940*), University of Thessaloniki, Thessaloniki 1942.

Oikonomou, A., *Φύση, τεχνολογία και κοινωνία στις ορεινές κοινότητες του Κιθαιρώνα* (*Nature, technology and society in the mountain communities of Kithairona*), Odysseas, Athens, 2007.

Oikonomou, K.E., *Τοπωνυμικό της περιοχής Ζαγορίου* (*Toponyms of the Zagori region*), PhD thesis, Scientific Yearbook of the *Dodoni* Philosophy Faculty, Appendix no. 45, Ioannina, University of Ioannina, 1991.

Papanastasis, V., "Λιβαδική αξία των δασών της βαλανιδιάς" ("Rangeland value of oak forests"), in *Δάση βαλανιδιάς: Παρελθόν, παρόν και μέλλον* (*Oak forests: Past, present and future*), Conference proceedings, T.E.I. Mesolongi - T.E.I. Lamia, Mesolongi 2002, pp. 47-52.

Petronotis, A. - Papageorgiou, V., *Μαστόροι χτίστες από τα Μαστοροχώρια της Κόνιτσας* (*Master builders from the Mastorochoria of Konitsa*), vol. 1, Ioannina Prefecture - Epirus A.E., Ioannina, 2008.

Psychogios, D.K., *Προίκες, φόροι, σταφίδα και ψωμί. Οικονομία και οικογένεια στην αγροτική Ελλάδα του 19ου αιώνα* (*Dowries, taxes, raisins and bread. Economy and family in agricultural Greece of the 19th century*), E.K.K.E., Athens 1995.

Rembelis, C., *Κονιτσιώτικα* (*Konitsa matters*), "I Proodos" Association of Asimochoritans in Athens, Athens 2005 (1st edition, Epirote Society of Athens, Athens 1953).

Rokou, V., *Ορεινές κοινωνίες κατά την περίοδο της οθωμανικής κυριαρχίας στα Βαλκάνια. Το Μέτσοβο της κτηνοτροφίας από τον 17ο έως τον 20ό αιώνα* (*Mountain societies during the period of Ottoman rule in the Balkans. Pastoralist Metsovo from the 17th to 20th century*), Erodios, Thessaloniki, 2007.

Seirinidou, V., "Οι ιστορικοί στη φύση. Μια εισαγωγή στην περιβαλλοντική ιστορία" ("Historians in nature. An introduction to environmental history"), *Istorika*, 51, 2009, pp. 275-297.

Siatras, D., *Αγοραπωλησίες ακινήτων στην τουρκοκρατούμενη Ελλάδα* (*Buying and selling of property in Ottoman Greece*), Gnosi, Athens, 1992.

Smyris, P., "Εισαγωγή: Το δασικό οικοσύστημα" ("Introduction: The forest ecosystem"), in Papageorgiou, A.H. - Karetsos, G. - Katsadorakis, G. (ed.), *Το δάσος. Μια ολοκληρωμένη προσέγγιση* (*Forest: A comprehensive study*), WWF Greece, Athens, 2012, pp.13-15.

Stara, K., *Μελέτη και καταγραφή ιερών δασών και δασυλλίων στον εθνικό δρυμό Βίκου-Αώου* (*Study and record of sacred forests and groves in the Vikos-Aoos National Park*), PhD thesis, University of Ioannina, 2009.

Stara, K. - Tsiakiris, R., "Τα λιβάδια που ήταν δάση. Η περίπτωση των προστατευτικών δασών του Ζαγορίου" ("The meadows that were forests: The case of the protected forests of the Zagori"), in Sidiropoulou, A., Mantzanas, K., Ispikoudis, I.

(eds.), *Πρακτικά 7ου Πανελληνίου Λιβαδοπονικού Συνεδρίου "Λιβαδοπονία και ποιότητα ζωής"* (*Proceedings of the 7th Panhellenic Rangeland Conference, "Rangeland and quality of life"*), Xanthi 14-16/10/2010, Thessaloniki, 2010, pp. 57-62.

Sugar, P., *Η Νοτιοανατολική Ευρώπη κάτω από Οθωμανική κυριαρχία (1354-1804)* (*Southeast Europe under Ottoman rule (1354-1804)*) , vols. 1 and 2, Athens, 1994.

Tsitsas, S.K., *Τ' αγριόδεντρα του βουνού και του λόγγου* (*The wild trees of the mountain and the* longos), Centre of Environmental Education in Mouzaki, Karditsa, 2009 (1st edition 1978).

Tsoupi, M., *Ηπειρώτικα λιθόγλυπτα. Τέχνη και κοινωνία. Ανιχνεύοντας στο Ζαγόρι* (*Epirote stone carving: Craft and society. Looking for traces in the Zagori*), Efyra, Ioannina 2006.

Vakalopoulos, A., *Ιστορία του Νέου Ελληνισμού* (*History of Modern Hellenism*), vol. 1., Thessaloniki, 1961.

Vergopoulos, K., *Το αγροτικό ζήτημα στην Ελλάδα* (*The agricultural question in Greece*), Exantas, Athens, 1975.

Berger J.- Luckmann T., *The social construction of reality,* Allen Lane, London, 1967.

Bloch, M., "The long term and the short term: The economic and political significance of the morality of kinship", J. Goody (ed.), *The character of kinship,* C.U.P., Cambridge, 1973, pp. 75-87.

Bourdieu P., *Outline of a Theory of Practice,* U.P. Cambridge, 1977.

Campbell J., *Honour, family and patronage*, Oxford U.P., 1964.

Croll E. -D. Parkin D.(eds), Bush base: Forest farm. Culture, environment and development, Routledge, London, 1992.

Eder K., *The social construction of nature,* Sage, London, 1996.

Fog Olwig K.- Hastrup K. (eds), Siting culture, Routledge, London, 1997.

Grove A.T.-Rackham O., *The Nature of Mediterranean Europe. An Ecological History,* Yale U.P., New Haven and London, 2001.

Gupta A. - Ferguson J. (eds), *Culture, power, place: Explorations in critical Anthropology,* Duke U.P ,Durham and London, 1997.

Halstead, P., "Ask the fellows who lop the hay: Leaf-fodder in the mountains of Northern Greece", *Rural History,* 9, 2, 1998, pp. 211-234.

Hirsch E.- O'Hanlon M., *The Anthropology of Landscape,* Clarendon, Oxford, 1995.

Ingold T., 1992, "Culture and the Perception of the Environment", in Croll E.-Perkin D. (eds), *Bush base: Forest farm. Culture, environment and development,* Routledge, London, 1992, pp.39-56.

Ingold T., *The Perception of the Environment,* Routledge, London, 2001.

Ingold T., *Hunters, pastoralists and ranchers,* U.P.,Cambridge, 1980.

Latour B., *We have never been modern,* Harvester/Wheatsheaf, New York, 1993.

Latour B., *The politics of nature: How to bring the sciences into democracy,* Cambridge Mass., 2004 (1st edition in French, 1999).

Low S.M. - Lawrence-Zuniga D., "Locating Culture" in Low S.M. - Lawrence-Zuniga D. (eds), *The Anthropology of Space and Place,* Blackwell, London, 2003, σελ. 1-47.

McGowan Br., *Economic life in Ottoman Europe (taxation, trade and the struggle for land, 1600-1800),* C.U.P- Maison des Sciences de l' Homme, Cambridge-Paris, 1981.

McNeill J.R., *The Mountains of the Mediterranean World,* U.P. Cambridge, 1992.

Milton K., *Environmentalism and Cultural Theory,* Routledge, London, 1996.

Sahlins P., *Culture and Practical Reason,* U.P. Chicago, 1976.

Stoianovich Tr., "Land tenure and the related sectors of the Balkan economy, 1600-1800", *Journal of Economic History,* XIII (1953), pp. 398-411.

Turner K. - Pearce D. - Bateman I., *Environmental economics,* Harvester Wheatsheaf, London, 1994.

UNESCO, *Environment and Society: Education and Public Awareness for Sustainability*. Proceedings of the Thessaloniki International Conference, 1997.

Urry J., *The Tourist gaze. Leisure and Travel in Contemporary Societies,* Sage, London, 2002.

APPENDIX

ILLUSTRATIONS

1. The landscape

2. The village

3. Kladero

4. *Field with kladero*

5. *Hut*

6. *Dried branvhes*

7. *Stable*

8. Kladaria

9. Ploughing

10. Stone-masons